OPTIONS FOR THE BEGINNER AND BEYOND

OPTIONS FOR THE BEGINNER AND BEYOND

UNLOCK THE OPPORTUNITIES AND MINIMIZE THE RISKS

W. Edward Olmstead

Professor of Applied Mathematics
McCormick School of Engineering and
Applied Sciences Northwestern University

Editor for *The Options Professor*
Published by Independent Investor, Inc.

Vice President, Publisher: Tim Moore
Associate Publisher and Director of Marketing: Amy Neidlinger
Executive Editor: Jim Boyd
Editorial Assistant: Susan Abraham
Development Editor: Russ Hall
Cover Designer: Chuti Prasertsith
Managing Editor: Gina Kanouse
Senior Project Editor: Kristy Hart
Copy Editor: Keith Cline
Senior Indexer: Cheryl Lenser
Compositor: Interactive Composition Corporation
Manufacturing Buyer: Dan Uhrig

FT Press offers excellent discounts on this book when ordered in quantity for bulk purchases or special sales. For more information, please contact U.S. Corporate and Government Sales, 1-800-382-3419, corpsales@pearsontechgroup.com. For sales outside the U.S., please contact International Sales at international@pearsoned.com.

Ninth Printing, November 2010

ISBN-10: 0-13-172128-3
ISBN-13: 978-0-13-172128-9

Pearson Education LTD.
Pearson Education Australia PTY, Limited.
Pearson Education Singapore, Pte. Ltd.
Pearson Education North Asia, Ltd.
Pearson Education Canada, Ltd.
Pearson Educatión de Mexico, S.A. de C.V.
Pearson Education—Japan
Pearson Education Malaysia, Pte. Ltd.

Library of Congress Cataloging-in-Publication Data

Olmstead, W. Edward.
  Options for the beginner and beyond : unlock the opportunities and minimize the risks / W. Edward Olmstead.
    p. cm.
  Includes index.
  ISBN 0-13-172128-3 (hardback)
  1. Options (Finance) 2. Investment analysis. I. Title.
  HG6024.A3O46 2006
  332.64'53—dc22

                                                        2005032449

To my wife Pandy, who gleaned enough
from the contents herein to become a
very proficient trader in her own right.
To my sons Hal and Randy, who
shared in my development as
an options trader.

CONTENTS

Section II: Trading Strategies 69

---

*Chapters with more advanced content are marked with an asterisk and can be passed over by
beginners during the first reading of this book.

ACKNOWLEDGMENTS

I am deeply indebted to Gregory Spear and Kathy Butler of Independent Investor, Inc., without whom *The Options Professor* newsletter and the contents of this book never would have been realized.

ABOUT THE AUTHOR

W. Edward Olmstead has a B.S. from Rice University and a Ph.D from Northwestern University, where he is currently Professor of Applied Mathematics in the McCormick School of Engineering and Applied Sciences. He has received several prestigious awards for teaching excellence, and has published extensively in engineering and applied mathematics journals.

In the world of finance, Dr. Olmstead has more than ten years of experience as an options trader. He also has taught courses that cover both the theory of options pricing and practical strategies for trading options. Since 2003, he has been the editor of *The Options Professor* newsletter published by Independent Investor, Inc. Presently, he also serves as an options analyst for Spear Capital Management. His consulting activities include work on short-term trading strategies for a member company of the Chicago Mercantile Exchange.

For more information about *The Options Professor* newsletter and seminars given by Dr. Olmstead, go to www.spearreport.com

PREFACE

This book is intended for people who are just starting to learn about options as well as for those who want to advance their basic knowledge to a higher level. Much of the material in this book has previously appeared in a series of articles written for *The Options Professor,* a monthly online newsletter about options trading, published by Independent Investor, Inc., Bloomfield, Connecticut. Some of the material was originally developed by the author for a course on options pricing theory taught at Northwestern University, Evanston, Illinois.

Section I includes Chapters 1 through 9. These chapters contain fundamental information about options, mainly intended for the beginner. Those who have some experience with options may still find it worthwhile to skim through Section I to fill some gaps in their knowledge.

Section II includes Chapters 10 through 25. Each chapter in this section is devoted to a strategy that goes beyond the basic trade of owning a call or a put option. Some chapters are an advanced continuation of the strategy introduced in the preceding chapter. The advanced chapters are marked with an asterisk and can be passed over by beginners during their first reading of this book.

Section III includes Chapters 26 through 30. Each chapter in this section covers a topic that is intended for people with options experience who want to develop a broader background. All of these chapters are marked with an asterisk, so this whole section can be passed over by beginners during their first reading of this book.

The method of exposition in this book is primarily through example. The options concepts in each chapter are introduced and discussed in the form of example trades. Many of the examples are illustrated with risk graphs, which serve to reinforce the concepts of each strategy.

All of the trades presented in the book are taken from real situations, although the prices may have been altered slightly to simplify the presentation. In most of the examples, the real stock symbol has been replaced by the mythical XYZ or ZYX, so that the reader can focus on the discussion without any distraction related to an experience with the actual stock. In some examples, the real stock symbols have been used because it seemed particularly important to the discussion.

Section I

BASIC CONCEPTS

Section I includes Chapters 1 through 9. These chapters contain fundamental information about options, mainly intended for the beginner. Those who have some experience with options may still find it worthwhile to skim through Section I to fill some gaps in their knowledge.

1

INTRODUCTION

Why Options?

Why should someone who invests or speculates in the market learn to use options? The simple answer is that options can greatly enhance your profit from stocks and/or provide the means to protect your portfolio. The goal of this chapter is to familiarize the beginner with call and put options, and demonstrate some of the basic ways that options are used.

Suppose you buy a stock for $30 a share and it goes to $33. The stock price has risen by 10 percent and accordingly you have a 10 percent profit. That's nice! If instead of buying the stock, you buy an appropriate option, you might make a 100 percent profit or even more for the same 10 percent rise in the stock price. That's better than nice. That's fantastic!

Of course, there are risks associated with options, just as there are risks with any investment. You need to understand the risks as well as the advantages of options in order to optimize your results.

Throughout this book, the use of call and put options are illustrated through a variety of examples. For simplicity, the focus is on equity options—that is, options associated with individual stocks. With minor variations, the same concepts apply to most other kinds of options, such as those associated with an index such as the Dow or those that represent an industry such as the semiconductor industry.

The Basic Concept of Options

To understand the basic concept of options, let's start with a simplified look at how they work.

An (equity) option is linked to a specific stock. The price of the option is much less than the price of the underlying stock, which is a major reason for the attractiveness of options. If the price of the stock changes, the price of the option will also change, although by a smaller amount. As the price of a stock goes through its daily ups and downs, the price of an associated option will undergo related fluctuations.

The price of an option can be viewed and followed in much the same way as a stock price. There are numerous online services, including the data feed for your brokerage account, that provide the prices of options. The Chicago Board Options Exchange (CBOE) offers a free online service for quotes on option prices that are 20 minutes delayed.

For a call option, if the stock price goes up, the option price also increases. If the stock price goes down, the price of the call decreases.

For a put option, if the stock price goes down, the option price increases. If the stock price goes up, the price of the put decreases.

This sounds like owning a call option is similar to holding a long position in the stock, because you have the potential to make a profit when the stock price goes up. And owning a put option is similar to holding a short position in the stock, because you have the potential to make a profit when the stock price goes down. In a rough sense, this analogy is true, but there are some significant differences.

Major Differences Between Stocks and Options

Leverage

Options typically cost only a fraction of the stock price. If you think XYZ stock, currently at $49 per share, is going up in price, you can purchase 100 shares at a cost of $4,900. If instead you buy 1 call option contract (1 contract represents 100 shares of stock), you might pay only $2 per share for a total of only $200 to participate in an upward price movement of XYZ.

Analogously, if you think XYZ is going down in price, you could short 100 shares of stock, but that creates a margin responsibility in your brokerage account, which can become costly if XYZ goes up. If instead you buy one put contract, you might pay just $2 per share for a total of only $200 to participate in a downward price movement of XYZ.

Time Limitation

One reason options are cheap is that they are time limited. A long or short position involving stock can be held indefinitely, but an option expires on a fixed date. The expiration date is typically the third Friday of the expiration month designated in the option contract. When you buy an option, you can select from various expiration months, including the current month as well as other months going out possibly as far as two years.

The longer you want to hold an option, the more expensive it will be. If a price of $1 per share applies to an option expiring in two months, a similar option expiring in four months might be priced at $2 per share. For 12 months, the price could be as much as $7 per share, but even this would typically be a small fraction of the stock price.

Another important aspect of being time limited is that the value of an option will decrease with time when there is no change in the stock price. If you buy an option for $1 per share with two months until expiration, for example, it might be worth only $.65 with one month to go if the stock price has not gone up. This is one of the risks of owning an option, namely that its value diminishes over time when the stock price remains unchanged.

Price Movement

As the stock price changes, the option price also changes, but by a lesser amount. How closely the change in the option price matches the change in the stock price depends on the reference price designated in the option contract. This reference price is called the *strike price*.

When you decide to purchase an option, there will be several strike prices from which to make a selection. For most stocks, the strike prices of its options are set at $5 increments within the broad trading range of the stock. For some lower- and medium-priced stocks, strike prices are offered in increments of $2.50, whereas options on some high-priced stocks only have strike price increments of $10.

There is a terminology used by options traders to describe the relative relationship between the stock price and the strike price of an option. If the strike price of either a call or a put is close to the price of the stock, the option is said to be *at-the-money*. If the strike price of a call (put) is above (below) the stock price, the option is said to be *out-of-the-money*. If the strike price of a call (put) is below (above) the stock price, the option is said to be *in-the-money*.

For an at-the-money option, the price of the option will change by about 50 percent of the amount of change in the stock price. For an out-of-the money option, the price of the option will change by less than 50 percent of the change in the stock price. The price of an in-the-money option will move by more than 50 percent of the change in the stock price.

For example, suppose XYZ stock is priced at $49 and a call option with a $50 strike price is purchased for $2 per share. If the price of XYZ stock rises by $2 up to $51 soon after purchasing the option, the price of the call would typically increase by about $1, raising its price by up to $3 per share. Suppose instead, a call option with a $55 strike price was purchased for $.75 per share. Then the same $2 move in the stock price might increase the price of the call by only $.20, up to $.95 per share. On the other hand, a call option with a $45 strike price and a cost of $5 per share might see an increase in the price of the call by as much as $1.60, up to $6.60 per share.

Of course, if XYZ fell $2 from $49 down to $47, the call option with a $50 strike price could be expected to lose about $1 per share, reducing its price from $2 down to $1. This illustrates how the leverage of options works in both directions.

Financial Risk

When you buy an option, your maximum risk is limited to your original cost of that option. The worst outcome is that you hold the option until expiration, at which time it has become worthless because the stock price failed to move in a beneficial manner.

For example, if you buy one option contract for a price of $2 per share, your cost is $200 ($2 \times 100 = 200$). This is the most that you can lose. Compare that dollar risk with the risk of either owning or shorting

100 shares of stock. When the stock price undergoes a substantial move against your long or short position in the stock, the dollar loss will be much greater than the cost of a call or put option.

A major risk with options is that you invest heavily by purchasing numerous contracts and then allow them to expire worthless. This represents a 100 percent loss on a significant investment. Of course, it is rarely necessary to lose all of your original investment when the stock does not move as expected. Typically, you can sell your options before expiration and recover some part of your original cost.

A Detailed Explanation of Options

Additional insight into options from both the owner and seller viewpoints is provided in the more detailed explanation that follows here.

The Option Contract

An (equity) option represents a contract between a buyer and a seller. This contract is an agreement concerning the buying or selling of a stock at a reference price during a stipulated time frame. You will never see any written document for this contract, just as you do not see actual shares of stock that you purchase in your brokerage account. The existence of the option contract is implied as soon as you buy or sell an option through your broker.

We will continually refer to the buying and selling of options. In case you are wondering where all this buying and selling takes place, there are exchanges for trading options similar to the exchanges for trading stocks. Your broker routes your order to buy or sell an option to one of those option exchanges, just like he sends your order to buy or sell stock to a stock exchange.

There are rights and obligations associated with an option contract, which need to be understood. Options associated with individual stocks trade in a manner called "American style," which permits the owner of the option to exercise the rights of the contract at any time before the option expires. To better comprehend the implications of an option being exercised, we examine the call option and the put option from the viewpoints of both the buyer (owner) and the seller (writer).

The Call Option

The buyer (owner) of a call option has the right to purchase 100 shares of stock at the strike price designated in the contract. This right to purchase can be exercised anytime before the contract expires. Typically, the time frame of the option extends through the third Friday of the expiration month stipulated in the contract.

The seller (writer) of a call option has the obligation to supply 100 shares of stock for purchase at the strike price, if so requested by the owner of the option. This obligation to supply the stock may be required at any time before the contract expires. As a practical matter, if the stock price is below the strike price, the stock is almost never "called" away from the seller. Even when the stock price goes above the strike price, the assignment of a call rarely happens until near the expiration date.

BUYING A CALL OPTION

The motivation to buy a call option could be based on your expectation that the price of XYZ stock will soon rise above its current level. Let's set up a possible trade, clarify its risk, and examine some possible outcomes resulting from the trade:

- **Trade.** In early February, with XYZ trading at $49, you decide to buy one call contract to benefit from the expected rise in the stock price. To allow a reasonable amount of time for XYZ to advance, you select a contract with an April expiration. You also select a strike price of $50. Option prices are quoted on a per-share basis, and let's suppose that this call option costs $2 per share. Because the option covers 100 shares of stock, this means you pay $200 to own this particular call contract.

  In the jargon of options, you are "long one XYZ Apr 50 call." Now you have the right to purchase 100 shares of XYZ stock at $50 per share anytime before the close of trading on the third Friday of April.

This right to purchase XYZ stock for $50 per share does not look so good at the moment, because the stock is priced in the market at only $49. Indeed, why have you paid $2 per share for something that presently has no intrinsic value? Because the expression "time is money" is most appropriate as it applies to options. You paid $2 per share as a cheap way to participate in the movement of the price of XYZ stock until the call expires in two months.

- **Risk.** Your risk on this trade is limited to the $200 paid for one call contract.

- **Outcome.** Let's examine a few scenarios to see how this trade might work out:

1. Suppose your faith in XYZ stock is validated as its price reaches $54 by the end of March. Now your right to purchase XYZ at $50 looks good, and you decide it is time to take your profit. Should you call your broker and tell him to exercise your right to purchase this stock at $50? No, because you will do much better if you just sell the option. The option you bought for $2 is likely to now be worth $5.50. So, the contract for which you paid $200 can now be sold for $550, giving you a nice $350 profit. That represents a 175 percent profit on the option, whereas the stock price has risen only 15 percent.

   Why is this option worth $5.50 when its intrinsic value is only $4 ($54 − 50 = 4$)? Again, because "time is money," and the person who buys your call option is paying the extra $1.50 per share over its intrinsic value in hopes that XYZ stock will go even higher before the April expiration.

   Let's see why selling the option is more profitable than exercising it. If you had exercised your option to buy XYZ stock at $50 and then immediately sold the stock at $54, that would be a $400 gain on the stock, less the $200 cost of the option for a net profit of only $200. So, exercising the option yields only a 100 percent profit as compared with the 175 percent profit received from selling the option. Also, selling the option avoids any issue about having enough cash in your brokerage account to take ownership of the stock.

2. In contrast to the happy Scenario 1, let's see what happens in the unfortunate case when XYZ is under $50 when the April options expiration date arrives. If you remained stubbornly optimistic until the end, you would have seen the value of your option diminish until it expired worthless. In this worst-case situation, you would lose all of the $200 that you originally paid for the option. Usually, there is no need to incur such a complete loss. If XYZ is still around $49 in early April with only a couple of weeks left until expiration, you might conclude that the chance for success looks remote. Then sell your option for whatever value remains. Suppose that you could sell the option for $1 per share and thereby close the trade for a 50 percent loss. The decision to limit your loss on a long option trade to 50 percent is a reasonable exit strategy.

SELLING A CALL OPTION

Suppose that you own 100 shares of ZYX stock, which at the current price of $67 is above where you bought it, but now seems to be stalled. It would be nice to make a bit more money on this stock, and you would be quite happy to part with it at $70 per share. This could be your motivation to sell a call. Selling a call would immediately bring some cash into your brokerage account, and if ultimately you are required to give up your stock for $70 per share, that is an additional gain. Let's set up a possible trade, clarify its risk, and examine some possible outcomes resulting from the trade:

- **Trade.** In early February, you decide to sell one call contract on ZYX. You pick the $70 strike price and a March expiration. The March option is selected so as to have an early resolution as to whether your stock will be retained or sold. Suppose that you are able to sell the March call for $2 per share. Because the contract covers 100 shares of stock, that brings in $200, which is yours to keep.

In the jargon of options, you are "short one ZYX Mar 70 call." Also, this particular combination of owning a stock and selling a call is referred to as a *covered call position.* Chapter 14, "Covered Calls," discusses this type of trade more fully.

You now have the obligation to give up your stock at $70 a share if someone exercises that right against you before the close of trading on the third Friday of March. Does this mean your stock will be called away as soon as its price is a penny over $70? No, because under most circumstances you only need worry about losing your stock within a few days of the expiration date. Why? As illustrated previously, until near the expiration date, the owner of the option will always profit more by selling it than by exercising it. Of course, as the expiration date is reached with ZYX above $70, someone is ultimately going to exercise their option and call away your stock.

■ **Risk.** Your risk here is the usual risk of owning a stock, because its price could drop significantly. To a small degree, this risk is offset by the decrease in value of the short call.

■ **Outcome.** Let's examine a few scenarios to see how this trade might work out:

1. At expiration, ZYX is at $71. Your stock is called away for $70. You have made $2 per share for the call that you sold, and the stock is being sold for $3 more than the $67 it was worth when you sold the option. Thus, you have a $500 gain since the time that you initiated the option trade.

   Things look a little different if ZYX is $74 at expiration. Your stock will still be taken away at $70, and you have exactly the same $500 gain that you had when ZYX closed at $71. But in this case, you could have made $700 on the stock if you had not sold the option. Of course, that $700 gain is unrealized unless you actually sell the stock at $74. One benefit of the covered call trade is that it forces some discipline upon you to take a profit and get rid of a stock that possibly has little upside left in it.

2. If ZYX is slightly above $70 as expiration nears, you might decide that you do not want to part with your stock. Then you must buy back the short call. If ZYX is hovering around $71 on the expiration day, you can probably buy back the call option for a bit more than $1 a share (even at expiration it will cost you a little more than its intrinsic value). This gives you a profit of the difference between the $2 that you took in from the sale of the call less your approximate cost of $1 from buying it back. Now you get to keep your stock, but if its price soon begins to fall, you may regret the decision to keep it.

3. If ZYX is only $69 at expiration, the call that you sold expires worthless. You already have the $2 from selling the option, and you also retain your stock. The cost basis for your stock has been lowered by $2 per share. Now you can repeat the process in the next month. If you were able to continue bringing in $200 every month with this covered call strategy, that represents a 36 percent annual return on a $67 stock that does not even need to go up in price. If the stock goes up gradually and each month you can sell a call at a higher strike price, things are even better.

4. Suppose that ZYX has pulled back to $64 at expiration. Now your stock has lost $3 per share from the time that you sold the call. This unpleasant situation is somewhat relieved by the $2 per share received for the call that you sold. In this case, your net loss is only $1 per share.

The Put Option

The buyer (owner) of a put option has the right to sell 100 shares of stock at the strike price designated in the contract. This right to sell can be exercised anytime before the contract expires. Typically, the time frame of the option extends through the third Friday of the expiration month stipulated in the contract.

The seller (writer) of a put option has the obligation to buy 100 shares of stock at the strike price, if so requested by the owner of the option.

This obligation to purchase the stock may be required at any time before the contract expires. As a practical matter, the stock is never "put" to seller if the stock price is above the strike price. Even if the stock price is below the strike price, the put assignment typically does not happen until near the expiration date.

BUYING A PUT OPTION

The motivation to buy a put option could be based on your expectation that the price of XYZ stock will soon fall from its current level. Let's set up a possible trade, clarify its risk, and examine some possible outcomes resulting from the trade:

- **Trade.** In early February, with XYZ trading at $39, you decide to buy one put contract to benefit from the expected fall in the stock price. Because you expect XYZ to decline following an earnings report in early March, you choose a March option. You also decide on a strike price of $40. Let's say this put option costs $3 per share. Because the option covers 100 shares of stock, this means that you pay $300 to become the owner of this particular put contract. You are now "long one XYZ Mar 40 put." This gives you the right to sell 100 shares of XYZ stock at $40 per share anytime before the close of trading on the third Friday of March. This right to sell at $40 per share is a slight improvement over its current price of $39; however, that gain of $1 per share is offset by the $3 per share paid for the option. Why have you paid $3 for something that has an intrinsic value of only $1? Again, "time is money," and you have paid an extra $2 per share of time value in order to play XYZ for a downward move until the put expires in March.

- **Risk.** Your risk on this trade is limited to the $300 paid for one put contract.

- **Outcome.** Let's examine a few scenarios to see how this trade might work out:

  1. The earnings report for XYZ is indeed weak and the stock sinks to $34. Now your right to sell XYZ at $40 per share looks good. Does it matter that you do not own any XYZ

stock to sell? No, because if you are ready to take your profit, all you need do is sell the option. The option you bought for $3 is likely to now be worth $7. So, the contract for which you paid $300 can now be sold for $700, giving you a nice $400 profit. That represents a 133 percent profit on the option, whereas the stock dropped only about 13 percent.

Why is the option worth $7 when its intrinsic value is only $6 (40 − 34 = 6)? As said before, time is money, and the person who buys your put option for $7 is paying an extra $1 per share over its intrinsic value in hopes that XYZ will go even lower before the March expiration.

Let's see why selling the option is better than exercising it. To assign the option, you would first need to buy the stock at $34 per share and then exercise your right to have someone buy the stock at $40 per share. Your gain would be $600 on the stock less the $300 you paid for the option, giving a net profit of only $300. So, exercising the option yields a 100 percent profit as compared with the 133 percent profit received from selling the option.

2. In contrast to the happy Scenario 1, let's see what happens in the case when the price of XYZ stock is still at $39 when the March options expiration date arrives. The earnings report failed to negatively impact the stock price and you have stubbornly refused to accept that outcome until the end. Then you would have seen the value of your option shrink from $3 down to its intrinsic value of $1. You could then sell the option for $100, which represents a $200 loss based on the $300 paid for the option.

SELLING A PUT OPTION

Suppose that you shorted 100 shares of ZYX stock when it was $65 a share. It has fallen to $62 in early February, but seems to be stalled at that price level. You do have a $300 profit, but your original goal was to ride this stock down to $60 for a profit of $500. This could be the motivation for selling a put option. Selling a put would immediately bring some cash into your brokerage account, and if ultimately you are required to close your short position at $60 per share, that is an additional gain. Let's set up a possible trade, clarify its risk, and examine some possible outcomes resulting from the trade:

- **Trade.** In February, you decide to sell a March contract so as to have an early resolution on the position of being short ZYX stock. You find that you can sell the March $60 put for $2 per share, which brings $200 into your brokerage account. You are now "short one Mar 60 put." This means that you might be required to buy 100 shares of ZYX at $60 per share at anytime before the March options expiration date. For all practical purposes, this is not going to happen unless ZYX is below $60 as the expiration date nears. If you are required to buy the stock at $60, your broker will immediately use those shares to close your short position in ZYX, which you initiated at $65.

- **Risk.** Your risk here is the usual risk of being short a stock, because its price could rise significantly. To a small degree, this risk is offset by the decrease in value of the short put.

- **Outcome.** Let's examine some scenarios to see how this trade might work out:

  1. Suppose that ZYX is still at $62 when the March expiration date arrives. Because the stock price is above the strike price at expiration, the option expires worthless. Now you can keep the $200 that you received from selling the put option and your short position in the stock remains in place. Thus, you have managed to make some additional profit on this short position, even though the stock is right where it was when you sold the put.

  2. If the price of ZYX is at $59 at expiration in March, you would be required to buy 100 shares of the stock at $60 per share. These purchased shares would immediately close your short position in ZYX. Now you have achieved your original goal of riding the stock down from $65 to $60, plus you have brought in an extra $2 per share from selling the put. This yields $500 from the short sale of the stock plus $200 from the option for a total profit of $700.

Comments

The discussion in this chapter focused only on some of the more common uses of call and put options. A variety of strategies use options in other ways to enhance the opportunity for making a profit under the appropriate circumstances. Many of those strategies are presented in this book.

Time is money. This phrase should always be in the back of your mind as you deal with options. Remember that the value of an option decreases in time when everything else remains unchanged. When you own an option, time is your enemy. When you have sold an option, time is your friend.

Before you can begin trading options, you need to consult your broker to determine what types of option trading will be allowed in your account. The types of allowed trades will depend on the size of your account as well as whether it is a retirement account. Upon receiving approval, you will be able to do options trading in your brokerage account much like you do stock trading, either by directing your broker to place orders or by online transactions done by yourself.

2

OPTION SELECTION

What Is a Cheap Option?

Each of us has our own idea about when something is cheap. On a superficial level, something that costs $1 is cheap, and something that costs $100 is expensive. But it is not really the dollar cost that makes something cheap or expensive. Rather, it is whether the intrinsic value of the item purchased is close to the cost paid to own that item. Often, we are tempted to buy something at a price which has been "hyped" way beyond its intrinsic value. Remember the Beanie Baby craze of a few years ago, when those cute little stuffed animals were being hyped as collector's items and as such were being bought for way more than their intrinsic value? Now that the craze has passed, these items are being sold at garage sales for a price that is much closer to their intrinsic value. The hype value of the Beanie Baby has disappeared over time.

What does this have to do with options? Well, every option has a price that represents its intrinsic value plus a hyped value. In the language of option traders, the hyped value of the option is called its *time value*. We are all familiar with the cliché "time is money," and never was this expression truer than as it applies to the price of an option. Options are time-limited financial instruments, and it makes sense that an option with a life of five months should cost more than an option with only one month of life. With any option, you do not want to pay for too much time value. One situation that warrants caution is when a stock is generating lots of excitement (good or bad), because the price of its options will be hyped up with extra time value.

Whenever you consider buying an option, it is a good idea to identify just how much of its price is intrinsic value and how much is time value. It is easy to compute its intrinsic value by asking this question: What would this option be worth if it expired immediately today? When that intrinsic value is deducted from the full option price, the remainder is the time value.

Let's look at a couple of examples:

■ **Example 1.** In mid-November, XYZ stock is at $89. The December 85 call gives you the right to purchase 100 shares of XYZ stock at $85 per share at anytime before this option expires in about four weeks. The asking price for this call is $4.50 per share. How much of this price is intrinsic value and how much is time value?

If this option were to expire as you are looking at it, you could exercise your right to buy XYZ at $85 and then sell it at the current market price of $89 for a profit of $4. So, the December 85 call has an intrinsic value of $4 per share. The rest of the price of the option is its time value, which in this example is $.50 per share [4.50 − 4.00 = .50].

Compare the December 85 call priced at $4.50 per share with the April 85 call priced at $7.50 per share. The intrinsic value is still $4, but for the April option, the time value has increased to $3.50 per share [7.5 − 4.0 = 3.5]. This illustrates that "time is money" because you will have to pay $3.50 per share to control this stock for five months as compared with $.50 per share to control it for four weeks.

■ **Example 2.** Again, XYZ is at $89 in mid-November. The December 90 call is priced at $1.50 per share. How much of this price is intrinsic value and how much is time value?

If this option were to expire as you are looking at it, it would be worthless. The right to buy XYZ for $90 per share is worthless when the stock can be bought in the open market for $89 per share. So, the December 90 call has an intrinsic value of $0. The rest of the price of the option is time value, which in this case is the total price of $1.50. If XYZ does not go up during the four weeks before the December 90 call expires, the value of this option will shrink to $0.

Now, let's get back to the original question: What is a cheap option? The XYZ December 85 call is $4.50 per share, while the December 90 call is only $1.50 per share. Is the December 90 call really cheaper? If we just consider time value, the December 90 call is three times more expensive than the December 85 call ($1.50 versus $.50). Of course, if XYZ is going to $95 before the December expiration in four weeks, you will have a much larger percentage profit if you bought the December 90 call. But suppose XYZ only edges up to $91 at the December expiration. The December 90 call would be worth $1 and you would have a loss of $.50 per share [1.00 − 1.50 = −.50]. Compare that with the December 85 call, which would be worth $6, and you would have a profit of $1.50 per share [6.00 − 4.50 = 1.50].

Now let's ask the same question—What is a cheap option?—in a different context. The XYZ April 85 call is $7.50 per share, while the December 85 call is only $4.50 per share. Is the December 85 call really cheaper? Although the time value of the April 85 call is much more than the December 85 call ($3.50 versus $.50), keep in mind that the April option has four extra months of life after the December option expires. It might seem expensive to buy that extra time value, but you are paying for a much longer window of opportunity to be right about a significant rise in XYZ stock. Of course, if your timing is impeccable and XYZ makes a run within the next four weeks, the December 85 call will yield a larger percentage profit than the April 85 call. But suppose XYZ goes nowhere before the December expiration, and then in January starts a leisurely climb to $95 by mid-March. In this scenario, the December 85 call expires with a loss of $.50 per share, whereas in mid-March with XYZ at $95, the April 85 call could easily be worth $11 per share for a profit of $3.50 per share [11.00 − 7.50 = 3.50].

The objective of this discussion is to start you thinking about intrinsic value and time value when you look at an option price. When you buy an option, you are almost always going to be paying for some time value—it is the nature of the beast. Just remember that for your option to make a profit, the stock price must move enough to overcome the loss of some if not all of that time value. The preceding examples demonstrate that the option with the lowest price is not always the best bargain.

Let's continue with the thought process that you should develop in selecting a particular call option or put option to buy. We will assume that you have identified a stock, which you think is going to make a move in price (either up or down). To play this expected move in the stock price, you decide to use options to achieve more leverage for profit. Now you need to determine which option is going to work best.

To select the best option, you need to examine various choices to arrive at a proper decision. In the following illustrations, we focus on the case in which the stock price is expected to go up and hence we want to buy a call option. At the end, you learn how a similar analysis can be applied to the case of buying a put when the stock price is expected to go down.

In the context of buying a call, three example choices are presented. For each example, we follow several scenarios to see whether the outcome is compatible with our expectations. The three examples do not cover every possible situation, but they should provide enough illustration for you to begin developing your own skills at analyzing outcomes.

Selecting a Call

When you buy a call option on a stock, you are taking the view that the stock is going to rise in price. You buy a call option instead of buying the stock to give yourself more leverage for a greater profit. If the stock goes up by 15 percent, your option might easily increase in value by 100 percent or even more.

After you have decided what stock you want to play for a gain, you need to select an appropriate call option to buy. This is not as simple as it might seem. You will have many possibilities from which to make a choice. There will be several expiration months to consider, including the current month and other months that possibly go out as far as two years into the future. You will also have various strike prices to consider, including ones below the stock price (in-the-money), near the stock price (at-the-money), and above the stock price (out-of-the-money).

Which option is best? To answer this question, you must decide what you believe will be the manner in which XYZ makes its upward move. Is this a stock that is going to jump up 15 percent in the next two weeks due to a much better than expected earnings announcement? Or, is this a stock that will slowly rise by 25 percent over the next year? As you review various choices of call options, think about how much the stock must rise and the time frame during which that rise must occur to produce a profit. Also, if the stock does not make the expected move up, check to see when you can exit the trade to minimize your loss.

General approach: When you consider buying a particular call option, first determine what portion of its total price is time value. Keep in mind that this time value will ultimately be lost as the option expiration date arrives. Then ask yourself, "Can the stock price rise high enough and fast enough to increase the value of this option by an amount that will offset the loss of its time value and provide an acceptable profit?" If you can answer yes to that question, you have a good reason to buy the option.

Let's look at some examples to illustrate this general approach. Some of the prices used in these examples have been estimated by using an options pricing calculator.

You think that XYZ is going to rise in price in the near to intermediate future. In early April, XYZ is at $67.

- **Example 3.** You consider buying the Apr 70 call, which is priced at $1.50 per share. This option seems cheap enough, but is it a good one to buy? To answer this question, let's see what XYZ needs to do for this option to provide a reasonable profit.

  The Apr 70 call expires in a little more than two weeks. Because this option is out-of-the-money, all of its $1.50 price is time value.

  If XYZ rockets up to $73 in one week, the option might become worth $3.70 ($3 intrinsic value and $.70 time value). This represents a nice $2.20 profit on a $1.50 investment, but it required a 9 percent gain in the stock price in one week.

  If XYZ only manages to rise gradually over the next two weeks to reach $71.50 just at expiration, the option will be worth $1.50 (all intrinsic value and no time value at expiration). In this scenario, XYZ has gone up by 7 percent in three weeks, but you only break even on the option trade.

  Suppose XYZ barely edges up to $68.50 with one week remaining. Then, this option might be worth only $1 (all time value), because it is still out-of-the-money and has only one week of life remaining. Now you have lost $.50 per share on the option even though the stock has moved up slightly, and there is almost no time left to recover.

Summary: This April option is cheap, but to make a nice profit, the stock needs to make a significant rise soon after the trade is initiated. This is not a likely scenario, which makes this trade quite risky.

- **Example 4.** You consider buying the May 65 call, which is priced at $4.20 per share. This option seems much more expensive than the Apr 70 call, but is that really true? Let's see what XYZ needs to do for this option to provide a reasonable profit.

  The May 65 call expires in seven weeks. Because this option is in-the-money, it has an intrinsic value of $2 [67 − 65 = 2]. Therefore, its time value is $2.20 [4.2 − 2.0 = 2.2]. In comparison with Example 1, we are paying for an extra $.70 of time value [2.2 − 1.5 = .7], but we have considerably more time for this option to return a reasonable profit.

  If XYZ is able to make the 9 percent gain to $73 in five to six weeks, this option might be worth $8.60 ($8 intrinsic value and $.60 time value). This represents a nice profit of $4.40 on a $4.20 investment. Although the percentage profit on this option trade is not quite as good as compared with Example 1, the May option has allowed more time for the stock to achieve its rise to $73.

  Suppose that XYZ does nothing for six weeks and then finally manages to move up to $71.50 in the seventh week just as expiration is reached. In this scenario, the option will be worth $6.50 (all intrinsic value and no time value at expiration). Here you have made a profit of $2.30 per share [6.5 − 4.2 = 2.3]. Compare this with Example 1, in which XYZ reached $71.50 at expiration and produced no profit.

  If XYZ is at $69.20 at the May options expiration, the May 65 call will be worth $4.20 [69.2 − 65 = 4.2] for break-even.

Summary: Although this May option may seem expensive, it has some important advantages. ~~By having a later expiration date, it gives the stock more time to make the desired move. By having a strike price that is in-the-money, the break-even point at expiration is lower.~~

- **Example 5.** You consider buying the Oct 65 call, which is priced at $8.30 per share. This option costs almost twice as much as the May 65 call in Example 4, but keep in mind that you are buying a lot more time. Let's see what XYZ needs to do to for this option to provide a reasonable profit.

The Oct 65 call expires in 27 weeks. Because this option has the same strike price of $65 as that of Example 2, its intrinsic value is the same $2 [67 − 65 = 2]. But this option has a time value of $6.30 [8.3 − 2.0 = 6.3]. In comparison with Example 2, we are paying for an extra $4.10 worth of time value [6.3 − 2.2 = 4.1], but we have an extra 20 weeks beyond the May expiration for this option to perform.

If XYZ is able to make a 9 percent gain to $73 in 18 weeks (about mid-August), this option might be worth $11 ($8 intrinsic value and $3 time value). This represents a profit of $2.70 on an $8.30 investment. Although the percentage profit on this option trade is not as good as compared with Examples 1 or 2, the October option has allowed considerably more time than either the April or May options to achieve its rise to $73.

Suppose that XYZ is able to make a 20 percent gain to $80 as the option nears expiration in October. Then the option will be worth $15 (all intrinsic value and no time value at expiration), and you will have made a profit of $6.70 on an $8.30 investment for an 81 percent gain. In this scenario, we have allowed almost seven months to achieve the 20 percent rise in XYZ. Such a rise would be much less likely in the shorter time spans described in Examples 1 or 2.

If XYZ is only at $70 in mid-September, this trade should be close to a break-even situation. At that time, you will have been able to follow the progress of XYZ for about 22 weeks. If the stock does not seem to be performing as expected, you could exit the trade without a loss.

Summary: This October option is the most expensive because it goes out the furthest in time and its strike price is in-the-money. The big advantage of this option is that it allows lots of time for the expected move in the price of XYZ to happen.

Overall Evaluation

Depending on the price action in XYZ stock, any of the Examples 3, 4, or 5 might produce the best profit.

Example 3 requires that you have impeccable timing about the move up in stock price. This super-aggressive trade is only going to pay off under special circumstances.

Example 4 illustrates the advantage of selecting an in-the-money option and allowing a little more time to be right about the stock price movement. This is a less-aggressive approach. If XYZ is a fairly volatile stock that cycles through a 10 percent to 15 percent move every few months, this could be the best choice.

Example 5 lends itself to a longer-term move up in the price of XYZ. This trade works best for a stock that is less volatile and more likely to show a steady upward growth over an extended time period. If LEAPS options are available, they would be a more-expensive choice that could extend the time frame out for two years.

Selecting a Put

When you buy a put option on a stock, you are taking the view that the stock is going to fall in price. You buy a put option instead of shorting the stock to give yourself more leverage for a greater profit.

The preceding examples illustrating the thought process in selecting a call option carry over to analogous examples for selecting a put. Different strike prices would be used for the corresponding puts, because an out-of-the-money put means the strike price is below the stock price, whereas an in-the-money put means the strike price is above the stock price.

Example 3 could be based on an Apr 65 put with similar option prices and profits resulting from analogous stock price movement down rather than up.

Examples 4 and 5 could be based on a May 70 put and Oct 70 put, respectively. Again, similar option prices and profits would follow from analogous stock price movement down rather than up.

3

ENTERING AND EXITING OPTION TRADES

O   ften, the success of an options trade is strongly influenced by
        how carefully the entry and exit prices are negotiated. The gain
        or loss of $.10 per share in a stock trade is usually insignificant,
whereas in an option trade it can make a huge difference. Suppose that
you buy an option for $2 per share and later sell it for $3 per share. The
profit of $1 per share represents a nice 50 percent return on your
investment. If you could have shaved your entry price by $.10 to $1.90
and managed to pad your exit price by $.10 to $3.10, your profit of
$1.20 per share represents a dramatically improved 63 percent return.

The point here is that, in options trading, it is very worthwhile for you
to work at achieving good entry and exit prices. Saving an extra $.10 on
either the entry price or the exit price of a trade is usually enough to
cover the brokerage fees on both ends of the trade.

To begin, let's review the basics of how options prices are maintained.

Nowadays, with the decimal pricing of stocks, the price of a stock is
shown down to $.01 changes. The situation with options is much dif-
ferent. Options that cost less than $3 per share can change price in
increments of $.05, but no smaller. Options that cost $3 per share or
more can change price in increments of $.10, but no smaller.

Each option exchange will list a bid price (called the bid) and an ask
price (called the ask) for every option that is available on a stock or

ask price - what you will pay to purchase.

index listed with that exchange. The bid is the highest per-share price that some trader (or market maker) is willing to pay to buy the option. The ask is the lowest per-share price that some trader (or market maker) is willing to accept for the purchase of an option. Most financial data feed services that provide options prices show only the best bid and best ask prices as selected from a survey of all the exchanges.

The ask is always greater than the bid, and the difference between these is called the bid/ask spread, or more simply the spread. Depending on the liquidity of the option, the spread may be as narrow as $.05 for options trading under $3 or as wide as $1 or more for some high-priced, illiquid options. Whenever the spread is wide enough, there is the possibility of negotiating a more favorable price somewhere between the bid and the ask.

The width of the spread for an option is essentially controlled by the market maker. He earns his living by managing an appropriate spread. His goal is to have someone buy an option from him at the ask, while someone else is willing to sell him the same option at the bid. The two option positions cancel each other, and the market maker pockets a profit equal to the value of the spread. This may seem like a small profit if the spread is only $.05 to $.10, but when repeated over a large number of contracts, it soon becomes quite substantial.

In a nonvolatile situation in which there is a high-volume demand for both buying and selling an option, the market maker is content with a narrow spread, because it is easy to match up his long and short positions while repeatedly collecting the value of the spread. In a highly volatile situation in which a large but unbalanced demand for an option exists, or in a low-volume situation, the market maker maintains a wide spread. In those situations, it is more difficult to find a matching trade, and the market maker wants a bigger spread to offset his risk.

Now let's turn our attention to the details of entering and exiting a trade. For simplicity, we confine our attention to the opening and closing of a long option position. That is, first buy an option in an "opening transaction" and then later sell the option in a "closing transaction."

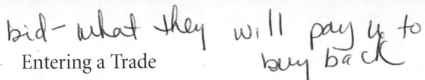
bid - what they will pay up to buy back

Entering a Trade

There are two main ways to initiate an "opening transaction" for an option. Similar to buying stock, the purchase of an option can be accomplished by means of either (1) a market order or (2) a limit order.

My recommendation is to never use a market order in an opening transaction. The best that you can do is to be filled at the ask price, and quite often you will do worse. If your order is for several contracts, you may find that only a few are filled at the ask before the price slides to a higher level for the remaining fills.

In a fast market where option prices are changing quickly, you may believe that you will only succeed in entering the trade by the use of a market order. In such a situation, you will be placing yourself at the mercy of the market maker, who is allowed considerable latitude in filling market orders during fast conditions.

So this leaves us with only the limit order as the principal way to initiate an option trade. With the limit order, you select the price that you believe is reasonable to pay for the option and enter that price with the order. There is no guarantee that your order will be filled, but if it is, it must be at your price or lower. Let's look at some examples to illustrate how to determine an appropriate price for a limit order to enter a trade:

- **Example 1A.** Bid = $2.40 and ask = $2.45. There is no room for negotiation here. The spread = $.05, which is the minimum possible for an option trading under $3 per share. Typically, the spread is this tight only for highly liquid options such as those associated with the NASDAQ 100 Trust (QQQQ). Place a limit order to buy at $2.45 and you should get a quick fill.

- **Example 2A.** Bid = $2.40 and ask = $2.80. With the spread = $.40, there is some room for negotiation. You could try to split the spread in the middle with a limit order to buy at $2.60. Getting filled at that price under slow conditions could be difficult. If you move the limit price up to $2.65 or $2.70, you are much more likely to get filled.

- **Example 3A.** Bid = $4.10 and ask = $4.40. Because the option is trading over $3 per share, the minimum spread would be $.10. Here the spread is $.30, which suggests that there may be some room for negotiation. You cannot split the difference at $4.15 because an option over $3.00 must be priced in $.10 increments. Typically, a limit order to buy at $4.20 is pointless, because you are asking the market maker to give up more than half the spread. A more realistic approach is to place a limit order at $4.30. This gives the market maker a $.20 spread, which should be enough to get the trade filled.

- **Example 4A.** Bid = $8.50 and ask = $9.10. With the spread = $.60, this is what you might see for a deep-in-the-money option that has no open interest. The market maker is not really interested in trading this option, but if you insist, he is going to make it worthwhile for himself. In this type of situation, be prepared to struggle to get a decent fill price.

Exiting a Trade

As it is with entering a trade, you can exit an option trade in a closing transaction by means of either (1) a market order or (2) a limit order. There are two additional ways to exit an option trade that are worthy of discussion, namely (3) a stop loss order and (4) a stop limit order.

I recommend never using a market order to exit a trade, except in extreme situations in which it seems imperative to exit a trade immediately to avoid substantial loss. Keep in mind that the fill price you receive on a market order to sell an option will not be any higher than the bid and will often be significantly lower.

As for a limit order, the situation is analogous to that of entering the trade. You select a price that you believe is reasonable to sell your long option and enter that price with the limit order. You may not get a fill, but if you do, it must be at that price or higher. Let's reexamine Examples 1A through 3A to illustrate how to determine an appropriate price for a limit order to exit a trade:

- **Example 1B.** Bid = $2.40 and ask = $2.45. Again, there is no room for negotiation here. The spread = $.05, which is the minimum possible for an option trading under $3 per share. Place a limit order to sell at $2.40 and you should get a quick fill.

- **Example 2B.** Bid = $2.40 and ask = $2.80. With the spread = $.40, there is some room for negotiation. You could try to split the spread in the middle with a limit order to sell at $2.60. Getting filled at that price under slow conditions could prove difficult. If you move the limit price down to $2.55 or $2.50, you are much more likely to get filled.

- **Example 3B.** Bid = $4.10 and ask = $4.40. Because the option is trading over $3 per share, the minimum spread would be $.10. Here the spread is $.30, which suggests that there may be some room for negotiation. You cannot split the difference at $4.15 because an option over $3 must be priced in $.10 increments. Typically, a limit order to sell at $4.30 is pointless, because you are asking the market maker to give up more than half the spread. A more realistic approach is to place a limit order at $4.20. This gives the market maker a $.20 spread, which should be enough to get the trade filled.

Next, let's examine the use of the stop loss order for selling an option. With this order, you indicate a trigger price at which you want the order to be initiated. The order to sell is then activated when either (1) the option trades at the trigger price or lower, or (2) the ask is at the trigger price or lower. When the order is activated, it becomes a market order to sell the option. As with a straight market order, this means the fill will not be any better than the bid when the order is activated and it may be substantially worse. My recommendation about using this type of order is only under extreme circumstances in which you are trying to avoid substantial loss.

Finally, let's consider the stop limit order for selling an option. As with a stop loss order, you indicate a trigger price at which you want the order to be initiated. But here you also indicate a limit price at which you want to sell your long option. The order is activated under the same two conditions previously described for the stop loss order. The difference here is that when the order is activated, it becomes a limit order to sell at the price you selected.

Getting filled on a stop limit order can prove tricky. You must carefully select your trigger price and your limit price to give yourself the best opportunity for a fill. If you set the limit price too close to the trigger price, you may not get a fill in circumstances in which you definitely want to be filled. Let's look at an example:

- **Example 1C.** You have a long call currently trading at $4. You want to try and protect this position with a stop limit order so that you will sell this option for no less than $3.50. Let's see what might happen if you set a trigger price of $3.60 and a limit price of $3.50. Suppose it occurs that the option price drops until the ask = $3.60 and the bid = $3.40. Because the ask has reflected your trigger price, your limit order to sell at $3.50 is then activated. Unfortunately, you will not get a fill here because the bid is lower than your limit price.

To avoid this situation, the gap between the trigger price and the limit price should be adjusted to reflect the anticipated bid/ask spread when the order is activated. In this example, it looks as if the trigger should have been set at $3.70 so as to account for the spread = $.20. Then, if the option price drops until the ask = $3.70 and the bid = $3.50, your order to sell will be activated with a limit price which is the same as the bid. This provides a much better chance of being filled at your desired price of $3.50.

4

THE GREEKS

As you learn about options and listen to the conversations of options traders, you will hear certain Greek letters mentioned. What are they talking about when they mention the delta, theta, gamma, vega (not a Greek letter), and rho? Are they referring to their favorite college fraternity or sorority?

The "Greeks," as they are called in the terminology of options trading, are one-word expressions used to describe how the price of an option changes when something else changes. The origin of this terminology lies in the theory of options pricing where these Greek letters were first introduced to define these price changes in exact mathematical statements. The main goal of this chapter is to provide an overview of the Greeks and their role in the trading of options.

Delta

The most basic and useful of the Greeks is the *delta*. Even with a simple working knowledge of the delta, you are immediately going to be a better options trader.

Delta: The amount that the price of an option changes as compared to a $1 increase in the stock price. This quantity is typically expressed as either a decimal or a percentage.

Computing the Delta of a Call Option

Let's illustrate with some examples:

- **Example 1.** XYZ is at $30 per share. The Mar 30 call, which expires in three weeks, is priced at $2 per share. Suppose the price of XYZ increases by $2 up to $32 per share. Typically, this will cause the price of the Mar 30 call to increase by $1 up to $3 per share.

Let's compute the delta for this Mar 30 call: Its price increased by $1 when the stock price increased by $2. Thus, the delta is given by the fraction 1/2 = .50, or 50 percent. So, a delta of .50 indicates that the price of the option increases by 50 percent the amount of the increase in the price of the stock.

This example illustrates an important basic property that holds for most options, namely, an at-the-money call (that is, strike price nearly the same as the stock price) typically has a delta of about .50.

- **Example 2.** XYZ is at $30 per share. The Mar 25 call, which expires in three weeks, is priced at $6 per share. Suppose the price of XYZ increases by $2 up to $32 per share. This might cause the price of the Mar 25 call to increase by $1.60 up to $7.60 per share.

  Let's compute the delta for this Mar 25 call: Its price increased by $1.60 when the stock priced increased by $2. Thus the delta is given by the fraction 1.6/2 = .80, or 80 percent.

  This example illustrates another basic property of options, namely, an in-the-money call (that is, strike price well below the stock price) will have a delta greater than .50 but less than 1.0. The deeper-in-the-money, the closer the delta will be to 1.0.

- **Example 3.** XYZ is at $30 per share. The Mar 35 call, which expires in three weeks, is priced at $.60 per share. Suppose the price of XYZ increases by $2 up to $32 per share. This might cause the price of the Mar 35 call to increase by $.20 up to $.80 per share.

  Let's compute the delta for this Mar 35 call: Its price increased by $.20 when the stock price increased by $2. Thus the delta is given by the fraction 0.2/2 = .10, or 10 percent.

  This example illustrates yet another basic property of options, namely an out-of-the-money call (that is, strike price well above the stock price) will have a delta less than .50. The further out-of the-money, the smaller will be the delta.

The delta values described in the preceding examples are typical for options that are not too close to expiration. Near-expiration, all in-the-money options will have a delta close to one, and all out-of-the-money will have a delta close to zero.

Application of the Delta

Now let's see how our experience with these three examples can help us with our options trading. You believe that the stock price of XYZ is going to increase in the near future and you want to play this move with options. What are you choices?

Buy an in-the-money call: If you want to capture an almost dollar-for-dollar increase in the price of the stock, you need to purchase an option with a high delta. This means selecting a deep-in-the-money call. If the option has a delta of .80, it will increase $.80 in price for every $1 increase in the price of XYZ. The deep-in-the-money call will be relatively expensive, but it will capture more of the price move in the stock.

Buy an at-the-money or out-of-the-money call: If you can count on a significant move in the stock within a short period of time, an at-the-money or out-of-the money call can yield a higher percentage increase in the price of the call. If the option has a delta of .50, a $2 increase in the price of XYZ will produce a $1 increase in the price of the option. If the option has delta of .20, a $2 increase the stock price will produce a $.40 increase in the price of the option. Because an at-the-money call will be relatively cheap and an out-of-the-money call will be even cheaper, these options offer more leverage for a profit.

At first glance, it might seem that you would always choose the at-the-money or out-of-the money call, because of the higher leverage. The real issue is whether the stock price will rise high enough and quickly enough for the extra leverage to yield a better profit. Suppose the trades in the above Examples 1, 2, and 3 were initiated when the March options were only three weeks from expiration. Also, suppose that XYZ waits until one week before expiration to make the $2 rise from $30 to $32. Let's follow up to see what might happen in the above examples.

- **Example 1 follow-up.** All the value of the Mar 30 call was time value. With only one week to go until expiration, its price could have fallen to $1, whereas its delta might still be .50. Then, the $2 move in XYZ would yield a $1 increase in the price of the option, bringing its value back to $2 per share for break-even.

- **Example 2 follow-up.** The Mar 25 call had only $1 of time value (25 + 6 − 30 = 1), so its price might have fallen to $5.40, with its delta remaining at .80. Then, the $2 move in XYZ would yield a $1.60 increase in the price of the option, bringing its value to $7 per share, for a net profit of $1 per share.

- **Example 3 follow-up.** All of the value of the Mar 35 call was time value. Being so far out-of-the money with only a week until expiration, its price might have dropped to $.15 a share with its delta remaining at .10. Then, the $2 move in XYZ would yield a $.20 increase in the price of the option, bringing its value to $.35 per share, for a net loss of $.25 per share.

What has been learned about the delta in these examples?

When considering an option to buy, make a mental estimate of the delta for that option. You do not necessarily need a precise value. Decide on a realistic increase in the price of the stock you are following. To estimate the new option price, first multiply the change in the stock price by the (approximate) delta of the option to see how much the value of the option would increase. Add that increase to the purchase price of the option, while allowing for some loss of time value in the option. If this estimate of the new price of the option represents an acceptable profit, you have a good reason to buy the option.

The delta of an option is not fixed. When the price of the stock moves significantly, the delta of an option will change. In Example 1, if XYZ moves up to $35, the Mar 30 call is no longer an at-the-money option. It has become an in-the-money option, and its delta will then be considerably larger. This works in your favor, because as the stock price rises to higher levels, the option price responds with a greater percentage of the stock gain.

Computing the Delta of a Put Option

The distinction between the delta for a call and the delta for a put is that the delta of a long put is always negative. This is because an increase in the stock price results in a decrease in the price of a put. Analogous to a call option, an at-the-money put generally has a delta of about –.50. An in-the-money put will have a delta between –.50 and –1.0. An out-of-the-money put will have a delta between –.5 and 0.

Theta

The next most commonly encountered Greek is the theta. The theta provides an estimate of how quickly your option is losing it time value.

Theta: The amount that the price of an option changes as compared to the passage of a unit of time (typically one day).

The value of theta is always a negative number, because the value of an option diminishes over time. In the terminology of options, the loss of time value is referred to as *theta decay.*

As a rough guide, the magnitude of theta for an at-the-money option varies inversely as the square root of the time remaining until expiration. For example, an option that has 40 days until expiration loses time value twice as fast as it did when it had 160 days until expiration [square root (160/40) = 2]. An option that has only 10 days until expiration loses value 6 times as fast as it did when it had 360 days until expiration [square root (360/10) = 6].

Some traders make a practice of never holding a long at-the-money option that has less than three weeks until expiration, because of the increasing rate at which the option will lose its value. With an out-of-the-money option, the situation can be even worse.

An easy way to get a rough measure of the theta of an option is to compare two options with the same strike price that have different expiration dates. For example, suppose your at-the-money option has a value of $4.30 per share with four months until expiration, whereas the option with the same strike price and only two months until expiration has a value of $2.50 per share. This means that, if the stock price remains unchanged over the next 60 days, your option will lose about $1.80 in value. That translates to a theta of approximately −$.03 per day [−1.80/60 = −.03], which may not seem like much until you recognize that it can add up to a 42 percent loss in the value of your option over the next two months.

Gamma

Gamma: The amount that the delta changes as compared to a $1 increase in the price of the stock.

The gamma becomes important in situations where the delta of an option becomes especially sensitive to changes in the price of the stock. Such situations are said to have *gamma risk*. One such scenario in which gamma becomes important occurs as an option approaches its expiration date.

As expiration gets close, the usual delta values of in-the-money and out-of-the-money options become distorted. All in-the-money options will have a delta closer to one, whereas all out-of-the-money options will have a delta that is closer to zero. So, a small increase in the stock price, from slightly below a strike price to slightly above it, will cause a change in the option delta from near zero to near one. This yields a large value of gamma. There is considerable risk in such situations, because a small decrease in the stock price can change a profitable call into one that is worthless.

Vega

The "vega" of an option provides a measure of its volatility. Just as stocks can be volatile, options can also be volatile, although there is not always a direct correlation of those volatilities. A stock whose price is volatile will typically have options with inflated prices, but it is also possible for options prices to inflate with little or no movement in the underlying stock price.

The point here is that each option has its own individual measure of volatility that is dictated by its particular price action. In options terminology, this individual volatility is called the *implied volatility*. The manner in which implied volatility is determined is discussed in Chapter 29, "Implied Volatility and the Black-Scholes Formula."

Vega: The amount that the price of an option changes as compared to a unit increase in the volatility of the stock.

The importance of vega is seen whenever circumstances surrounding the stock become excited for any one of a variety of reasons. Rumors that a stock might be bought out will quickly inflate the prices of the options associated with the stock. Under such a scenario, there can be a large increase in the price of an option even if the stock price changes little. This gives rise to a high vega.

Rho

Rho: The amount that the price of an option changes as compared to a unit increase in the risk-free interest rate (that is, the rate for a U.S. treasury bill).

Rho is positive for calls and negative for puts. With interest rates at the relatively modest levels seen in recent years, the influence on the price of options is slight.

5

RISK GRAPHS

A n ancient Chinese proverb declares: "One picture is worth more than ten thousand words." And so it is with understanding options trading. Because the value of an option depends on several factors, it is difficult to visualize the variety of ways its price can change without some kind of chart. The chart used to track the progress of an options trade is called a risk graph.

To follow the price movement of a specific option, the two factors of primary importance are the price of the underlying stock and the time remaining until expiration. The risk graph provides the visual means to comprehend how the profit or loss in an options trade is affected by changes in stock price as well as changes in time.

Risk graphs are used liberally throughout this book as a supplemental tool for visualizing the detailed workings of an options trade. These graphs are generated by a special calculator based on the Black-Scholes formula for pricing options, which is discussed in Chapter 29, "Implied Volatility and the Black-Scholes Formula." It is not necessary to understand how this calculator works, but only to accept that it does an excellent job in generating accurate options pricing data.

Basically, the risk graph is a two-dimensional plot of stock price versus the profit or loss in the options trade. In this book, the modern style of presentation is used, where the stock price is shown on the vertical scale and the profit or loss in the trade is displayed on the horizontal scale. (The old-fashion style of presentation interchanges these vertical and horizontal scales.)

Note that it is not an option price shown on the horizontal scale of the risk graph, because many risk graphs involve more than one option. It is much more convenient to have those options prices converted into a net profit or loss figure for display purposes. This allows the observer to easily identify the desired price range of the stock for achieving a profit on the trade.

To illustrate how the progression of time influences a trade, four time lines are displayed on each risk graph. One of the time lines always represents the current state of the trade. If the trade has just been initiated, that time line is the current state. Another time line always provides the projected profit or loss information at expiration. The other two time lines provide the projected state of the trade at times between the current state and expiration.

Single Option Trade

Let's look at an example of a risk graph to illustrate a trade involving a single long call:

- **Example 1.** This example recalls Example 3 from Chapter 2, "Option Selection." We use a risk graph to demonstrate how the information provided in that example was determined.

    You think that XYZ is going to rise in price in the near to intermediate future. In early April, XYZ is at $67.

    You buy 1 Apr 70 call, which is priced at $1.50 per share.

See Figure 5-1 for the risk graph that depicts this trade of being a long one XYZ Apr 70 call with 17 days until the option expires.

In Figure 5-1, the price of XYZ stock is shown on the vertical axis. On the horizontal axis is the profit or loss in the value of the option, with the zero point dividing the profit and loss regimes. The trade at the time of initiation is represented by the line labeled as "today: 17 days left." The time line representing the trade at expiration is labeled as "Expiry: 0 days left." In between are additional time lines for "12 days left" and "6 days left."

This option seems cheap enough, but is it a good one to buy? To answer this question, let's see what XYZ needs to do for this option to provide a reasonable profit.

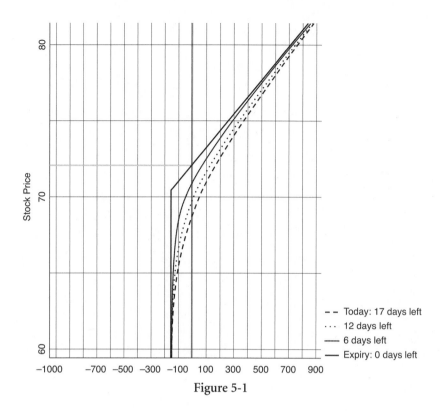

Figure 5-1

The Apr 70 call expires in a little over two weeks. Because this option is out-of-the-money, all of its $1.50 price is time value.

If XYZ rockets up to $73 in one week, the option might become worth $3.70 ($3 intrinsic value and $.70 time value). This represents a nice $2.20 profit on a $1.50 investment, but it required a 9 percent gain in the stock price in one week.

This profit information is found from the risk graph by moving horizontally along the stock price line for $73 until a point is reached, between the 6 days and 12 days time lines, which would represent 10 days left. Dropping down from that point to the horizontal axis indicates a profit in the trade of approximately $220. Because this trade involves only one Apr 70 call contract purchased for $150, this implies an option price of $3.70 per share [(150 + 220)/100 = 3.7].

If XYZ only manages to rise gradually over the next two weeks to reach $71.50 just at expiration, the option will be worth $1.50 (all intrinsic value and no time value at expiration). In this scenario, XYZ has gone up by 7 percent in three weeks, but you only break even on the option trade.

This information is found from the risk graph by noting that the time line at expiration crosses the zero profit axis at $71.50.

Suppose XYZ barely edges up to $68.50 with one week remaining. Then, this option might be worth only $1 (all time value), because it is still out-of-the-money and has only one week of life remaining. Now you have lost $.50 per share on the option even though the stock has moved up slightly, and there is almost no time left to recover.

This information is found from the risk graph by moving horizontally along the stock price line for $68.50 until a point is reached just to the right of the 6 days time line. Dropping down from that point to the horizontal axis indicates a loss in the trade of approximately $50. This implies an option price of $1 per share $[(150 - 50)/100 = 1.0]$.

Multiple Option Trade

Next, let's consider a trade involving two options. One option will be a long call that expires in a distant month, and the other option will be a short call in a near month. Both options have the same strike price. This type of trade is known as a *calendar spread*.

■ **Example 2.** This example of a calendar spread is presented and discussed in Chapter 12, "Calendar Spreads." Our goal here is just to look at the risk graph and see how to read it.

The stock price of XYZ is expected to trade within a narrow range around $35 for the next several months. In early May with XYZ at $34.70, the following trade is initiated. You buy 1 Nov 35 call for $3.50 per share and sell 1 Jun 35 call for $1.30 per share. Your net cost and maximum risk on this trade is $220 $[(3.50 - 1.30) \times 100 = 220]$.

See Figure 5-2 for a risk graph that depicts this calendar trade.

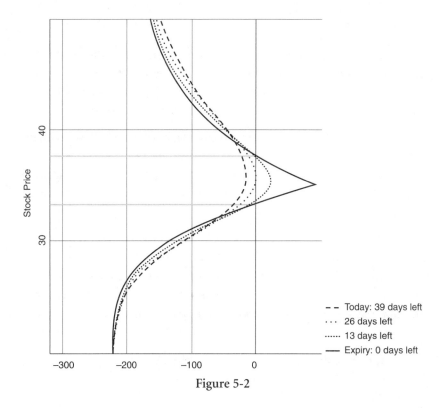

Figure 5-2

In Figure 5-2, note that on the day this trade is initiated, it is shown to expire in 39 days. This is reflecting that the Jun 35 call will expire 39 days after the date it is sold in early May. The Nov 35 call does not expire for another 150 days following the June expiration. This illustrates an important feature of risk graphs. They are only valid up until the expiration date of the earliest expiring option. To follow the progress of the trade after that date requires the calculation of a new risk graph.

From Figure 5-2, it is easy to see where you would like the price of XYZ stock to be when the Jun 35 call expires. The time line representing the trade at the June expiration date crosses the zero profit axis at $33 and $38. Thus, this calendar trade returns a profit at the June expiration if the price of XYZ is between $33 and $38 with a maximum profit of $90 if the stock price is exactly $35.

Comments

Even for a single option trade like that of Example 1, a risk graph can prove useful in making decisions about exiting a trade. Knowing that the option will achieve a profit only if the stock price rises by a certain amount before a particular date can be crucial information.

For trades with multiple options, particularly where the options have different expiration dates, the risk graph provides information that is very difficult to otherwise determine. In Example 2, the existence of a profit zone between $33 and $38 would be a mystery without the benefit of the risk graph.

Note in both of the examples that the point on the initial time line corresponding to the stock price at the time of entry lies slightly to the left of the zero profit axis. That is, as soon as the trade is entered, it is showing a small loss. This is known as *slippage*. It results from the difference between the bid and ask prices for an option, which was discussed in Chapter 3, "Entering and Exiting Option Trades."

Risk graphs can also be adjusted to reflect the influence of other factors that affect the price of an option. Most notable are the changes in the risk graph due to a significant change in the volatility of the option prices.

6

LEAPS

S ome stocks and indexes have options with expiration dates that occur two to three years into the future. These options are called LEAPS, which is an acronym for *Long-term Equity AnticiPation Securities.* Most LEAPS expire in January of their designated expiration year. These options include both calls and puts that function in the same manner as options associated with more-current expiration dates. Of course, these long-term options are relatively expensive because of their greatly extended lifetime.

You can use LEAPS in numerous ways. We discuss some of those uses here, while pointing out both the advantages and disadvantages of LEAPS. Because there can be drawbacks to using these long-term options, you should always "Look before you LEAPS."

One of the more popular uses of LEAPS is as a substitute for a buy-and-hold stock. In fact, LEAPS are sometimes referred to as the *poor man's stock.* This is because they can be purchased for a fraction of the cost of stock and then held for a long period of time.

To explore this concept of using a LEAPS call as a stock surrogate, let's look at an example in which we compare the performances of the option and the stock.

In early December 2004, XYZ stock is trading near $98 per share. If we buy 100 shares of stock, the cost is $9,800. Suppose instead, we buy a LEAPS call that will expire in about 25 months.

    Trade: Buy 1 Jan (07) 100 call option for $11.50 per share.

    Cost = $1,150.

    Max risk = $1,150.

See Figure 6-1 for a risk graph that depicts this trade.

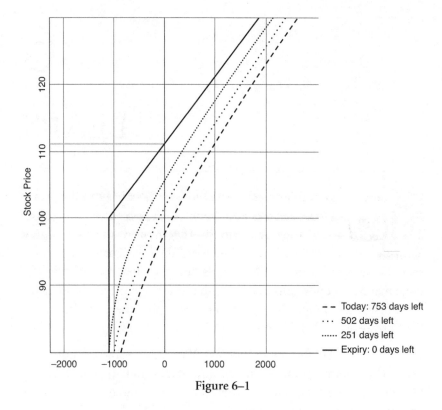

Figure 6–1

For a cost that is only 12 percent the cost of owning the stock, we can participate in the price movement of 100 shares of XYZ until the third Friday of January 2007, which is a little more than 2 years in the future. This sounds like a fantastic deal, and under the right circumstances it can be fantastic. But there are also circumstances in which it may not be advantageous to own the LEAPS call in place of the stock.

Now let's look ahead to some possible outcomes after 8 months and after 17 months:

- **Scenario 1.** After 8 months

  XYZ is at $120 for a 22 percent gain in stock value. The Jan (07) 100 call will show a profit of about $1,400, for a 122 percent gain in value. This dramatically illustrates the leverage of LEAPS options.

XYZ is at $110, for a 12 percent gain in stock value. The Jan (07) 100 call will show a profit of about $600, for a 52 percent gain in value. The LEAPS call is still providing a fantastic return.

XYZ is at $104, for a 6 percent gain in stock value. The Jan (07) 100 call will show a profit of about $90, for an 8 percent gain in value. The LEAPS call is slightly better.

XYZ is at $100 for a 2 percent gain in stock value. The Jan (07) 100 call will show a loss of about $100, for a 9 percent drop in value. This illustrates that even a LEAPS call experiences some loss in time value over the first eight months of its lifetime.

XYZ is at $95, for a 3 percent loss in stock value. The Jan (07) 100 call will show a loss of about $500, for a 43 percent drop in value. Here the LEAPS call has suffered a more dramatic loss of value because the stock price is significantly below the strike price of the option.

You can see the results for Scenario 1 in Figure 6-1 by looking near the line for 502 days left.

- **Scenario 2.** After 17 months

XYZ is at $120, for a 22 percent gain in stock value. The Jan (07) 100 call will show a profit of about $1,200, for a 104 percent gain in value. The return on the LEAPS call is still dramatically better after a full year.

XYZ is at $110, for a 12 percent gain in stock value. The Jan (07) 100 call will show a profit of about $400, for a 35 percent gain in value. Again, the LEAPS call provides a much better return.

XYZ is at $105, for a 7 percent gain in stock value. The Jan (07) 100 call will be nearly at a break-even status. After a full year, the LEAPS call has suffered enough loss of time value to offset a small gain in its intrinsic value.

XYZ is at $100, for a 2 percent gain in stock value. The Jan (07) 100 call will show a loss of about $300, for a 26 percent drop in value. The time decay over an additional 9 months has increased the loss of value in the option from 9 percent to 26 percent.

XYZ is at $95, for a 3 percent loss in stock value. The Jan (07) 100 call will show a loss of about $700, for a 61 percent drop in value. After a full year, a relatively small drop in the stock price results in a large loss of value in the LEAPS call, even though the option still has another year remaining in its lifetime.

You can see these results for Scenario 2 in Figure 6-1 by looking near the line for 251 days left.

The main lesson to be learned from the preceding example is that a LEAPS call performs much differently than stock. If the stock performs well, the LEAPS call will provide a greatly enhanced return. On the other hand, if the stock price gains little or experiences a small drop during the first quarter or first half of the LEAPS lifetime, the call option will perform poorly. The option may even suffer a loss while the stock makes a small gain, and it can suffer a substantial loss even if the stock has only a small drop in price.

In the preceding example, no illustration of performance has been shown when the stock price has fallen by a large amount after 8 months or 17 months. It is assumed that some stop loss feature is in place for either the stock or the option that would mitigate that situation. It is worthwhile, however, to note that if a catastrophic collapse of the stock price occurs, the dollar amount at risk with 100 shares of stock greatly exceeds that of one LEAPS call.

As a further illustration of the performance of LEAPS calls in comparison with stock, let's look at some actual results. On January 15, 2004, a group of 10 long-term options trades were issued to subscribers of *The Options Professor Newsletter* (a product of Independent Investor, Inc). The Options Medley 2004 consisted of 10 LEAPS Jan (05) calls based on 10 stocks drawn from a broad range of market interests. These options trades were designed to be aggressive, because they were using LEAPS that had only a one-year lifetime and whose strike prices were about 10 percent out-of-the-money.

When it was recommended that the Medley trades be closed on December 28, 2004, the total return was 121 percent, even though not all of the 10 trades were profitable. Here are actual results of two trades from the Medley, selected to illustrate one trade that was profitable and one that was not.

- **D.R. Horton (DHI).** The stock price was at $26 on January 15, 2004, when the Jan (05) 30 call was purchased for $2.80 per share. On March 3, 2004, DHI was at $33, for a 27 percent gain in the stock price. The LEAPS call was priced at $5.80, for a gain of 108 percent. By December 28, 2004, DHI was near $40, for a 54 percent gain in the stock price. The LEAPS call was priced at $9.60, for a gain of 243 percent.

- **Verizon Communications (VZ).** The stock price was at $37 on January 15, 2004, when the Jan (05) 40 call was purchased for $1.70 per share. When this trade was closed on December 28, 2004, VZ was near $41, for an 11 percent gain. The LEAPS call was priced at $1.20, for a loss of 29 percent.

The Medley concept illustrates an important aspect of using LEAPS calls instead of buying stock. For the same cost as owning 100 shares of a single stock, it is possible to participate in the price movement of 100 shares of several stocks by buying LEAPS calls, thereby spreading risk across a diversified portfolio.

Another trading strategy that uses LEAPS calls involves the selling of front-month premium against the long-term calls. This is similar to the covered call strategy, which is discussed later in Chapter 14, "Covered Calls." In the previous example with the XYZ Jan (07) 100 call, you could begin by selling the Feb (05) 105 call for $.50 per share, which brings $50 cash credit into your brokerage account. If this could be repeated on a month-by-month basis, it would generate $600 over a 12-month period. This would substantially offset the loss situations described in Scenario 2. Of course, this strategy could lead to situations in which profit from the upward movement of the stock price would be limited by the short call.

The use of both LEAPS calls and puts is essential to the collar trade strategy. This strategy is also discussed later in Chapter 18, "Collars," and Chapter 19, "Advanced Collars."

Comments

Some remarks are in order regarding the role of dividends when LEAPS calls are used in place of stock. Unlike owning the stock, the owner of a LEAPS call does not receive any dividend distributed by the company. You must take this into account when comparing the performance of the option with the stock. In the previous example with XYZ, if the annual yield from dividends issued to stockholders is less than 1 percent, the performance comparisons shown previously are essentially unaffected. If XYZ paid annual dividends of 6 percent, however, this would significantly influence the performance comparison.

7

ASSIGNMENT ANXIETY

O ne thing that causes anxiety for beginning options traders is the prospect of receiving an assignment on an option that they have sold. The goal in this chapter is to relieve some of the anxiety about this aspect of options trading.

In this chapter, it is assumed that you do not have a naked short call or a naked short put position. If you do, you are entirely justified in being anxious, because you are vulnerable to substantial risk. Only experienced options traders should venture into naked option trading. This aspect of options trading is discussed later in Chapter 20, "Naked Option Writing," and Chapter 21, "Stock Substitutes."

So, it is assumed here that your short option position is covered by either long stock or a long option position. By having a compensating stock or option position, you will be well placed to emerge from an assignment with only limited loss or even possibly a profit depending on the circumstances of the trade. This chapter uses a variety of examples to clarify your thinking about the possibility of an assignment.

To begin, let's look at the typical circumstances under which you might be subjected to an early option assignment (that is, an option is exercised against you before the expiration date of the option):

Guideline 1: If the short option is out-of-the-money, you will (essentially) never receive an assignment.

To understand why this is true, consider these examples:

- **Example 1**. In early November, the price of XYZ stock is $38, and you are short the Nov 40 call. Someone who wants to own XYZ stock is not going to exercise his right to buy the stock from you at $40 per share, because he can buy the stock in the market for only $38 per share.

- **Example 2**. In early November, the price of XYZ stock is $38, and you are short the Nov 35 put. Someone who wants to sell his XYZ stock is not going to exercise his right to make you buy his stock at $35 per share when he can sell it in the market for $38 per share.

Guideline 2: If the option is in-the-money, there is not going to be an early assignment as long as there is sufficient time value included in the price of the option.

To illustrate this concept, consider these examples:

- **Example 3**. In early November, the price of XYZ stock is $41, and you are short the Nov 40 call, which is currently being bid at $2. You are not going to receive an assignment when the option price includes time value of $1 [2.0 − (41 − 40) = 1.0]. If the person who holds the Nov 40 call wants to own the stock, he is much better off buying the stock in the market for $41 and selling his call to someone else for $2. If he did require you to sell him your stock at $40, it is true that he would save $1 per share on the purchase price of the stock, but he would give up the opportunity to collect $2 per share by selling his option.

- **Example 4**. In early November, the price of XYZ stock is $34, and you are short the Nov 35 put, which is currently being bid at $2. You are not going to receive an assignment when there is time value of $1 [2.0 − (35 − 34) = 1.0]. If the person who holds the Nov 35 put wants to get rid of his stock, he is much better off selling the stock in the market for $34 and selling his put to someone else for $2. If he did require you to buy his stock at $35, it is true that he would gain $1 per share on the sale price of the stock, but he would give up the opportunity to collect $2 per share by selling his option.

Guideline 3: When the expiration date of a short option is close and the time value of an in-the-money option has almost disappeared, the possibility of an early assignment becomes much more likely.

Let's reexamine Examples 3 and 4 in the last few days before the November expiration date:

- **Example 5.** One week before the November options expire, the price of XYZ is $41. You are short the Nov 40 call, which is currently bid at $1.10. With time value of only $.10 [1.10 − (41 − 40) = .10], there is a real possibility of an early assignment. Someone who wants to own this stock may decide that the extra $.10 per share that could be gained from buying the stock and selling the option is not worth the trouble.

- **Example 6.** One week before the November options expire, the price of XYZ is $34. You are short the Nov 35 put, which is currently bid at $1.10. With time value of only $.10 [1.10 − (35 − 34) = .10], there is a real possibility of an early assignment. Someone who wants to get rid of his stock may decide that the extra $.10 per share that could be gained from selling the stock and selling the option is not worth the trouble.

Comments

Examples 1 and 2 suggest that an early assignment is not going to occur when there is $1 (or more) of time value, whereas Examples 3 and 4 suggest that you should be prepared for an early assignment when the time value is $.10 (or less). As a general guideline, the dividing point between these two outcomes is about $.15 to $.20 of time value. If the bid price of the option includes at least $.20 of time value, an early assignment is rather unlikely. If the bid price of the option includes no more than $.15 of time value, the possibility of an early assignment is more likely.

In comparing the scenarios of Examples 5 and 6, the early assignment of the put option happens more often than the early assignment of the call option. Someone who wants to get rid of his stock via an assignment is usually in a rush to get the cash from the sale and move on to a new investment. Someone who is considering buying the stock via an assignment is more likely to postpone the purchase as long as possible so as to avoid committing the cash until absolutely necessary.

The possibility of an early assignment can sometimes depend on a dividend payment. You may be more susceptible to the early assignment of a short call from someone who wants to collect an upcoming dividend. You may be less susceptible to an early assignment of a short put from someone who wants to wait for the dividend payment before selling his stock.

Whenever your short option becomes deep-in-the-money, there will be very little time value in the bid price of the option, even if the expiration date is far into the future. This situation makes early assignment a definite possibility.

If you judge that your situation is such that an early assignment is a possibility, check the open interest (number of outstanding contracts) on your option. A low level of open interest makes an early assignment more likely.

Applications

Now let's look at some situations involving either a covered call trade or a spread trade. In a covered call trade, your short option is hedged by stock that you own. In a spread trade, your short option is hedged by a long option.

- **Example 7.** Covered call. You own 100 shares of XYZ stock, and you have sold one Nov 40 call for $2.50 per share. As long as the stock price is below $40, as in Example 1, you have no concern about early assignment. Even when the stock price is above $40, there is no concern if there is sufficient time value in the option price, as in Example 3. Only when the stock price is above $40 and the time value included in the option price falls to $.15 or less do you need to worry about an early assignment, as in Example 5.

In a covered call trade, if an early assignment becomes a real possibility, you must decide on a course of action:

1. You can elect to do nothing, in which case your stock eventually will be bought from you at the strike price of the short option. This need not be viewed as an undesirable outcome. You get to keep the cash received from the sale of the short call, and you might be taking a profit on a stock that is soon due for a pullback.

2. You can elect to "roll out" of your short call. In Example 5, you can buy back the Nov 40 call and then sell a Dec 45 call. This will allow your stock to run to the $45 level until the December options expiration date.

- **Example 8. Bull call spread.** Being bullish on XYZ stock, you buy one Nov 35 call for $4.70 per share and sell one Nov 40 call for $2.50 per share. This represents a net cost of $220 [(4.70 – 2.50) × 100 = 220]. If XYZ is above $40 at expiration, the spread should ideally be showing a profit of $280 [(40 – 35) × 100 – 220 = 280]. Suppose that as the November expiration arrives, XYZ is trading at $41. You will often find that if you try to exit the spread by buying back the Nov 40 call and then selling the Nov 35 call, you will only be able to bring in something like $4.80 per share rather than the expected $5 per share. This is due to the slippage in the bid and ask prices on the options. To get the full $5, allow your short Nov 40 call to be assigned, while you exercise your right of the Nov 35 call to buy the stock at $35. So XYZ stock will be bought at exactly $35 and then sold at exactly $40, giving you the $5 difference that you deserve.

- **Example 9. Calendar spread.** XYZ is trading near $40 and the front-month options seem to have extra time value, so you decide to capture some of that premium through a calendar spread. You buy one Jan 40 call for $4 per share and sell one Nov 35 call for $2.50 per share for a net cost of $150 [(4.00 – 2.50) × 100 = 150]. Soon after you initiate this trade, it is announced that XYZ is being bought by another company for

$50 per share. As a result of this situation, you will find that both the Nov 40 call and the Jan 40 call are priced close to $10 per share with essentially no time value. You are likely to soon be assigned on your short call. The easiest way to counteract this assignment is to exercise your right of the Jan 40 call to buy XYZ at $40 per share. So XYZ stock will be bought at $40 per share and sold at $40 per share. Your loss on this calendar spread is limited to the original cost of $150 to initiate the trade.

8

BROKER SELECTION

To enhance your success at trading options, it is important that you give careful consideration to your choice of a brokerage firm. If you were only going to trade stocks, there are plenty of brokers whose services are adequate. To trade options, you must be more selective in picking a broker.

All brokers claim that they are "options friendly," but you need to examine their services closely to see whether this claim is justified. The goal here is to outline elements of broker services that are most important to options trading.

Types of Brokers

For purposes of this discussion, we refer to three types of brokers: full service, discount, and options specialty.

Although your broker should address all of your investment needs, you need to check that their options service is suitable for your purposes. You do not necessarily need an options specialty broker, but you should review the various items discussed in this chapter to make sure that your broker is truly options friendly.

Commissions

If you are going to trade options on a regular basis, you should be concerned about commissions. Because commissions on options trades are always higher than on similar stock trades, it is worthwhile to pick a broker who offers a reasonable rate.

With some full-service brokers, the commissions are so expensive that your potential to make a profit is significantly diminished. Until recently, even the so-called discount brokers were charging relatively high commissions on options trades. Fortunately, this is changing as several of the big-name discount brokers have reduced their commissions to be more competitive with the options specialty firms.

Nowadays, there is no need to use a broker who is charging $2 per contract along with a ticket charge of $15 or more. Some of the top-notch discount brokers, who offer almost as many benefits as the full service brokers, have reduced their commission rates to $1 or less per contract along with a $10 ticket charge.

Essentially, all of the options specialty brokers charge $1.50 or less per contract with a ticket charge of $7.50 to $10. Some now apply only one ticket charge for a multi-leg options trade. This is a great savings for those who do a lot of spread trading.

All brokerage firms charge more for phone orders handled by one of the brokers on their staff. It is worthwhile to get the lower commission rate by learning to place your options trades online. With a little practice, you will soon be better at initiating options trades than many of the broker staff.

Trading Platform

When you do your own trades online, you definitely want a high-quality trading platform. This is essential to getting good entry and exit prices for your options trades.

Most brokers offer some kind of free trial examination of their trading platform. You should take advantage of such an offer to see whether a particular platform seems options friendly.

The most important feature is that you have real-time stock and option quotes. In today's market, things move way too fast for you to be making decisions based on delayed quotes.

Your platform should provide a convenient means to view option chains, where you can quickly and easily identify the various strike prices and expiration months. Good platforms also show you the volume and open interest numbers for each option. The best platforms additionally provide deltas and implied volatilities for the options.

A good platform enables you to trade directly from the option chain. You can simply highlight the option of interest and bring up a window to execute the trade. The best platforms also show you the bid/ask prices at each options exchange and enable you to direct your trade to the exchange of your choice.

Good platforms provide stock charting on several time frames, including daily and one-minute intervals. These platforms also offer a variety of tools (moving averages, stochastic oscillators, and so on) that can be added to the charts. The best platforms enable you to simultaneously view several charts with different time frames. Being able to follow minute-by-minute stock movement can prove helpful in selecting entry and exit points for your options trades.

Most brokers do not charge for the use of their trading platform, provided that you do a sufficient number of trades per month. If your trading activity falls below the required level, a nominal monthly charge applies.

The best platforms for options trades enable you to enter multi-leg trades as a single entry. A few brokers even have platforms that allow contingent option orders, whereby an option trade can be triggered by the price action in the underlying stock.

Margin and Trading Limitations

Margin requirements vary markedly from one brokerage firm to another. Also, wide variations exist among brokers as to the types of allowed options trades, particularly in retirement accounts.

The most restrictive brokers require margin that corresponds to the worst-case scenario for every option in your account, regardless of other options in the account that ensure a hedged position. The most liberal brokers only require margin on short option positions to the extent that they are not appropriately hedged.

An easy way to get an overall sense of a broker's policy on margin requirements is to inquire whether they require margin on butterfly trades. (Chapter 23, "Butterfly Spreads," discusses this type of trade.) It does not matter whether you plan to do butterfly trades. The answer to this one question will provide a good gauge of the broker's policy on margin. The more restrictive brokers do require margin on butterflies, whereas the most liberal brokers do not.

In most cases, the options trading restrictions imposed by a broker relate to their policy on margin. This connection becomes quite apparent in retirement accounts. The most restrictive brokers forbid all spread trades in retirement accounts, as well as any option trade that might require margin. The most liberal brokers allow almost any option trade for which there is sufficient cash and/or equity in the account to close the trade if necessary.

Live Broker Assistance

Sooner or later, the time will come when you urgently need the assistance of a live broker. Almost all brokerage firms provide a phone number to connect you with some kind of live assistance, but the quality of that assistance varies dramatically from one firm to another.

The first issue is how quickly you can get through to live assistance. Being on hold for 10 minutes could prove costly when trying to resolve a sensitive trade problem.

The second issue is the competence level of the person who takes your call.

Many brokerage firms have a severely limited staff of people who are thoroughly familiar with options trades. When you need help with an options trade, you want someone on the line who understands your problem. Good brokers provide you with direct access to a team of brokers who specialize in assistance with options trades.

In principle, the options specialty brokers should be the best at providing competent assistance. Although this is true for many of them, there are some whose access to a live broker is restricted.

Comments

If you are going to be trading options on a regular basis, it is important to be able to execute your trades in the most convenient and cost-effective manner. Picking a brokerage firm that is truly options friendly will go a long way toward achieving that goal.

9

MISCELLANEOUS TIPS

H ere are some miscellaneous tips to help you become more successful in trading options. Some of these have already been suggested in earlier chapters, but are worthy of repeating here for emphasis.

Time Is Money

The expression "time is money" is one of the most important concepts in options trading. It is most relevant to those who either own an option or are planning to buy an option.

If you own an option, time is your enemy. You must keep in mind that the time value of your option will diminish, particularly during the last two to three weeks before expiration. If your option is out-of-the-money, you are especially vulnerable to a total loss of investment in the trade. Never hold an out-of-the-money option until the very end with only the faint hope that unforeseen circumstances will cause the stock to move favorably for you. An early exit from a few of these hopeless trades can salvage enough capital to fully finance a new trade. Forget about those rare instances in which the stock did finally move favorably during expiration week, because those highly infrequent payoffs will not offset several trades with a 100 percent loss.

When you are considering an option to buy, make sure that you allow enough time to be proven right in your judgment about the stock. It may be tempting to select that cheap front-month option on a stock that you expect to soon move up, but three to four weeks can pass very quickly. The option with the same strike price that expires two to three months later may seem expensive, but it is usually worth paying more to get the extra time to participate in the expected stock movement.

Trading with the Trend

Before initiating an option trade, check the current trend of your stock as well as the overall trend in the market. Because option trades are time limited, make sure that the trend is working with you.

It is usually not wise to take an option position that attempts to capture a bottom or a top in the stock price. Wait for some confirmation of the move you want to capture. You can afford to be patient about entering a trade, because, with the leverage of options, you do not need to catch much of a move in the stock to make a nice profit.

If the stock you like has pulled back, look for a clear indication that it has resumed its uptrend before buying a call. If the overall market has been in a bearish mode, be careful about initiating a bullish option trade until a reversal seems evident.

Risk Capital for Options Trading

Beginning options traders often ask, "How much of my total trading capital should I devote to options trading?" To answer this question, you must decide how much of your total investment capital you are willing to use for high-risk trading. This individual decision depends on many factors, not the least of which is your tolerance for risk. If you are conservative, allot no more than 10 percent of your total investment capital for trading options.

After you have decided on an amount that you feel comfortable using for high-risk trading, commit only about 15 percent of that amount to any single options trade. For example, if you initially decide that of your $50,000 trading capital, you can devote $5,000 toward trading options, risk no more than about $750 in any individual trade.

In the very beginning, limit yourself to only two to three trades that are open at the same time. As you gain confidence, you can increase that up to five to six trades, which at 15 percent per trade would involve essentially all of your allowed high-risk capital. It is wise to always keep a little cash in reserve for special purposes.

As you become more knowledgeable about options, you can devote a larger portion of your total trading capital toward trades that use options. For example, you can begin to use long-term options (LEAPS if available) as a substitute for stock, even in some of the more conservative portions of your portfolio. Also you may want to use put options as a low-cost insurance for your total portfolio.

Tracking Trades

It is important for you to acquire an appreciation for the progress of your trades over time. You need to develop a feel for the change in the price of an option as the underlying stock price changes and as time passes. The best way to achieve this is to systematically track your trades.

After you have initiated a trade, begin a tracking process. You can do this either in a spreadsheet or simply by hand with a sheet of paper. Enter the symbol for the underlying stock at the left end of the first row and immediately to the right indicate the price of the stock when the trade was entered. On the row below, just under the stock symbol, enter the option that you have purchased along with the number of contracts (for example, 5 Nov 20 calls). Immediately to the right, enter the price per share paid for the option, which should line up just under the stock price at the time of purchase.

Then, on a regular schedule, record the prices of the stock and the option in horizontal rows while moving from left to right across the page. Each new entry will show the current price of the stock in the first row and the corresponding price of the option in the row just below it. These log entries can be done as frequently as day by day or as infrequently as once a week, depending on how closely the trade needs monitoring. To keep track of the passage of time, you can occasionally enter a date next to the stock and option prices recorded on that day.

This tracking process will provide you with a record of how your trade is progressing over time. By following this record, you will soon develop a good sense of two basic option properties: (1) the response of the option price to a change in the stock price, and (2) the decay in the value of the option as the expiration date is neared.

After you have some experience with this record-keeping process, you will be able to make a very good guess of the option price as soon as you have seen the stock price. This tracking process will help you to develop a keen sense of when to exit a trade.

Anticipating Events

It is important to keep abreast of any upcoming events that concern the stock associated with your option trade. Any event that might have a significant influence on the stock price has the potential to produce a huge change in the price of a related option.

Of course, some events cannot be anticipated, but there are many that can be. Perhaps the most important event for any stock is the quarterly earnings report. Also, dates for stock splits and dividends are important. These dates are known well in advance and can be easily found on free Web sites (for example, Yahoo! Financial). Less-common events such as a drug approval or a court decision may not have a specifically announced date, but the likely time may be known within a couple of weeks.

If you are tracking your trades as suggested, you can enter the important dates as part of the log process.

Real-Time Quotes

Nowadays, it is fairly easy to obtain cheap, if not free, streaming quotes of stock and options prices in real time. Many of the major brokerage firms offer this data free to customers who are even mildly active traders. Access to real-time price data is very important for entering and exiting option trades. By watching option prices in real time, you can make a more intelligent decision about executing a trade at the best price available.

Market Orders with Options

Don't use them except in extreme circumstances. If you enter a market order to buy or sell an option, you will very frequently be disappointed with the fill. It is usually worth the extra trouble to enter a limit order, monitor the price movement of the option, and then adjust the limit price if necessary to get filled at a fair price.

Options Calculator

This is something you should consider as soon as you have developed some preliminary experience with options trades. Many traders now rely on an options calculator to evaluate a potential trade before they initiate it. These calculators can do a variety of things to help you make an informed decision about a trade. They can estimate the profit or loss in an option trade that would exist for any price of the underlying stock at any time before the expiration date of an option. They can compute the probability of your trade being profitable based on the volatility of the underlying stock.

The most useful options calculators generate a visual image in the form of a risk graph, as seen in Chapter 5, "Risk Graphs". These risk graphs are particularly useful when evaluating a trade that involves multiple options and more than one expiration month.

Unfortunately, many of the best options calculators come with a hefty price tag. Some of the options friendly brokers provide a free options calculator as part of their data feed service.

If nothing else, these options calculators can save you from initiating a trade that has little chance for success. Avoid a few hopeless trades and you have justified paying for a calculator.

Section II

TRADING STRATEGIES

Section II includes Chapters 10 through 25. Each chapter in this section is devoted to a strategy that goes beyond the basic trade of owning a call or a put option. Some chapters are an advanced continuation of the strategy introduced in the preceding chapter. These chapters are marked with an asterisk and can be passed over by beginners during their first reading of this book.

Section II

TRADING STRATEGIES

10

VERTICAL SPREADS

The most basic option trade is to buy a call or a put depending on which way you think the underlying stock is going to move. The next stage of options trading is the use of spreads. In the simplest spread trade, you buy one option and sell another in order to reduce the cost of the trade. There are a variety of spread trades, which are discussed in this book. The focus of this chapter is on vertical spread trades. Of all the spread trades, these are perhaps the easiest to implement and to follow.

What does a vertical spread offer beyond just buying a call or a put? The simple answer is that a vertical spread may offer an improved opportunity for profit with reduced risk.

A vertical spread can be one of two basic types: a debit vertical spread or a credit vertical spread. Furthermore, each of these basic types can be structured as either a bullish or bearish trade. A debit spread is typically used when you expect the stock movement to occur over an intermediate to long-term period of time, whereas a credit spread is typically used when you want to take advantage of a short-term situation.

Let's look individually at each of these vertical spread trades to see how they work and when you might use them. We will illustrate each of the four vertical spreads, which are commonly referred to as Bull Call Spread, Bear Put Spread, Bull Put Spread, Bear Call Spread.

Debit Vertical Spreads

Bull Call Spread

During July, you decide that XYZ is going to make a significant move up over the next four months going into the fall of the year. XYZ is currently at $35 per share, and you feel it will be at $40 or higher by November.

To play this expected rise in XYZ with options, you consider buying a Nov 35 call for $4.10 per share. But this is an expensive option, when you recognize that all of the $4.10 is time value. Suppose that XYZ barely reaches $40 just as this option expires in November. In this situation, the Nov 35 call option would only be worth $5 per share. This represents a profit of just $.90 per share [5.0 − 4.1 = 0.9], for a return of just 22 percent on your original risk of $410 per contract.

To lower the risk, consider a bull call spread.

> Trade: Buy 1 Nov 35 call for $4.10 per share and sell 1 Nov 40 call for $2.10 per share. This represents a net debit of $2 per share.
>
> Cost = $200 [(4.10 − 2.10) × 100 = 200].
>
> Max risk = $200.

Suppose that XYZ is $40 (or higher) at the November options expiration. Because all the time value in both options will have vanished, the difference in their prices will be equal to the difference in the strike prices, or $5 in this example. Thus, you will have a profit of $3 per share [5.0 − 2.0 = 3.0], for a return of 150 percent on your original risk of $200 per contract.

See Figure 10-1 for a risk graph that depicts this trade.

Bear Put Spread

During July, you decide that XYZ has no more upside and should fall back to a lower level over the next four months. With XYZ currently at $35, you judge that it will drop to the $30 level or lower by next fall.

To play this drop in XYZ with options, you consider buying a Nov 35 put for $3.90 per share. Again, this is an expensive option, because you are buying only time value. Suppose that XYZ barely falls to $30 as this option expires in November. This option could only be sold for $5 per share for a profit of $1.10 per share [5.0 − 3.9 = 1.10]. This represents just a 28 percent profit on your original risk of $390 per contract.

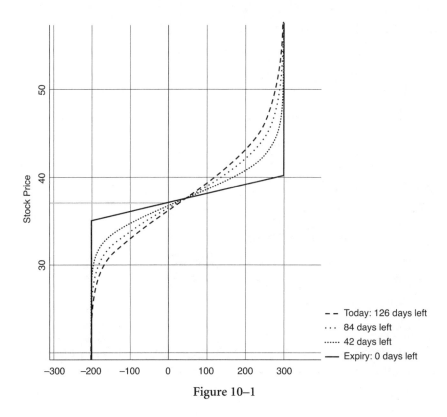

Stock Price

- – Today: 126 days left
- ⋯ 84 days left
- ⋯⋯ 42 days left
- — Expiry: 0 days left

Figure 10–1

To lower the risk, consider a bear put spread.

> Trade: Buy 1 Nov 35 put for $3.90 per share and sell 1 Nov 30 put for $1.80 per share. This represents a net debit of $2.10 per share.
>
> Cost = $210[(3.9 − 1.8) × 100 = 210].
>
> Max risk = $210.

Now, suppose that your negative view of XYZ is correct and the stock is at $30 at the November options expiration. Because all the time value in both options will have vanished, the difference in their prices will be equal to the difference in the strike prices, or $5 in this example. Thus, you will have a profit of $2.90 per share [5.0 − 2.1 = 2.9], for a return of 138 percent on your original risk of $210 per contract.

See Figure 10-2 for a risk graph that depicts this trade.

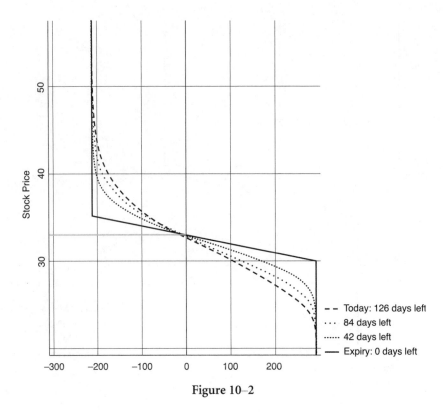

Figure 10-2

Comments

The bull call spread and the bear put spread are debit spreads. For these trades to pay off, the stock needs to have enough time to move to the targeted level. For this reason, you want to use options with expiration months that allow enough time for this move to occur.

To achieve the maximum profit, the stock price needs to have reached (or exceeded) the strike price of the short option at expiration. The maximum possible profit is always the difference between the strike prices of the long and short options less the original cost of the spread.

Typically, you need to wait until near expiration to get the best payoff from a debit spread. This allows the short option to lose all of its time value. If the stock reaches (or exceeds) the target price well before the options expire, the spread will show a profit that is usually much less than the maximum.

Credit Vertical Spreads

Bull Put Spread

You feel that current circumstances surrounding ZYX are likely to drive up the price of ZYX in the near future. ZYX is currently at $45, and you feel that it will surpass its recent high of $50 before the May options expire in six weeks.

This scenario can be played with a bull put spread.

> Trade: Buy 1 May 45 put for $2.70 per share and sell 1 May 50 put for $5.30 per share. This produces a net credit of $2.60 per share.
>
> Credit = $260.
>
> Max risk = $240.

If ZYX is above $50 at the May options expiration, both options will expire worthless and the initial credit of $260 will be yours to keep. This is the maximum possible profit on the trade. In the case of credit trades, the return is calculated from comparing the profit achieved to the maximum risk, or 108 percent in this example [(260/240) = 1.08].

The maximum loss of $240 occurs if ZYX is below $45 at the May expiration date. In this situation, both options must be closed at a cost equal to the difference in the strike prices, or $5 in this example. [(2.6 − 5.0) × 100 = −240]

See Figure 10-3 for a risk graph that depicts this trade.

Bear Call Spread

Due to some weakening of the economy, you foresee a dramatic fall in the price of ZYX in the near future. With ZYX currently at $45, you judge that it will fall back to its recent low of $40 by mid-May.

This scenario can be played with a bear call spread.

> Trade: Buy 1 May 45 call for $3 per share and sell 1 May 40 call for $5.70 per share. This produces a net credit of $2.70 per share.
>
> Credit = $270.
>
> Max risk = $230.

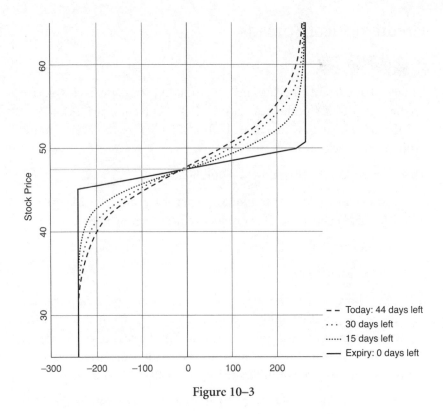

Figure 10–3

If ZYX is below $40 at the May options expiration, both options will expire worthless and the initial credit of $270 will be yours to keep. This is the maximum possible profit on this trade. The profit achieved as compared to the maximum risk on this trade is 117 percent $[(270/230) = 1.17]$.

The maximum loss of $230 occurs if ZYX is above $45 at the May expiration date. In this situation, both options must be closed at a cost of the difference between the two strike prices, or $5 in this example. $[(2.7 - 5.0) \times 100 = -230]$.

See Figure 10-4 for a risk graph that depicts this trade.

Comments

The bull put spread and the bear call spread are credit spreads. These trades bring money into your account, which ultimately becomes a

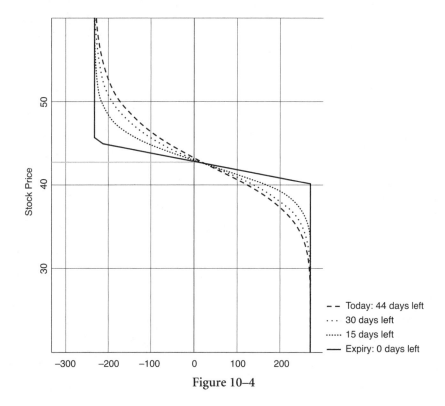

Figure 10–4

profit if the stock price reaches (or exceeds) the targeted level at expiration. These trades are typically short-term trades that seek to capture the credit as soon as reasonably possible.

As in the case of debit spreads, the maximum profit is achieved if the stock price reaches (or exceeds) the strike price of the short option at expiration. The maximum profit is the amount of the original credit.

Also, as in the case of debit spreads, the maximum profit will typically be realized at expiration. Credit spreads enjoy an advantage over debit spreads in that, when their target is reached, no action is required at expiration. Both options expire worthless.

11*

EVENT-PRODUCING CREDIT SPREADS

T o further illustrate vertical spread trades, this chapter explores an idea for finding good credit spreads with options. We indicate when to enter the credit spread and how to structure it.

First let's review the three major elements that typically characterize a good vertical credit spread:

1. A credit spread works best when extra premium has been pumped into the price of the option being sold.

2. A good credit spread is structured so that the underlying stock price needs little or no movement to achieve maximum profit.

3. Conditions are such that 1 and 2 can be realized using front-month options.

Now let's see when we might expect to find the circumstances that would give rise to 1, 2, and 3.

Look for an event that produces a major move in the price of a stock price accompanied by exceptionally high volume. This can be a move up or down in price. Most important, the cause for this major move must be an event that is essentially concluded after the news is out. We want to see a dramatic move in the stock price followed by a relatively short period of time in which the stock price stabilizes or slightly reverses the big move. This kind of situation pumps lots of extra time value into the front-month options as traders scramble to cover existing positions or attempt to ride the momentum wave in the hope that a second burst will follow.

The idea is to not enter the credit spread until the dust has had a chance to settle. The aim is to place the short leg of the spread near the extreme price attained during the dramatic move. This may require careful observation for a few days in case there is another surge that needs to exhaust itself.

What kind of events might produce the desired scenario:

- **A major earnings surprise.** Once announced, there is nothing else to be said about earnings for the immediate future. It may take a couple of days for stock traders to unravel their positions, but then the story is over.

- **Government approval or disapproval of a product.** This often describes a well-publicized drug that has been awaiting an FDA ruling for testing or marketing. After the decision has been made, the effect on the company profits is calculated, and the price moves to reflect the revised view of stock value. This is the end of story for the immediate future.

- **A proposed buyout** (particularly when viewed as a buyout that might not ultimately occur). The stock price gaps up to reflect the suggested buyout price, but then begins to pull back as the likelihood of the buyout begins to be questioned.

Let's look at some examples of setting up a credit spread following a special event:

- **Example 1.** Rambus, Inc (RMBS). On February 12, 2004, it was announced that European patent officials had revoked a patent claim by RMBS. This meant that the company would not be able to collect on a large amount of royalty fees from competitors in certain global markets. On huge volume, the stock quickly fell from the $30 level to close at $24.35.

  The bad news was out and the damage was done. This was a one-time type of event that was not likely to lead to any further related bad news. The big drop on huge volume suggested that the sellers had completed expressing their feelings. The chart on RMBS provided additional evidence that the stock had bottomed because of strong support at $24 going back to November 2003. The next day the stock began a little rebound back to the $25 level. This was a good opportunity to initiate the following credit spread:

Trade: Buy 1 Mar 22.5 put and sell 1 Mar 25 put for a net credit of $1.25 per share.

Credit = $125.

Max risk = $125 [(25 − 22.5 − 1.25) × 100 = 125].

See Figure 11-1 for a risk graph that depicts this trade.

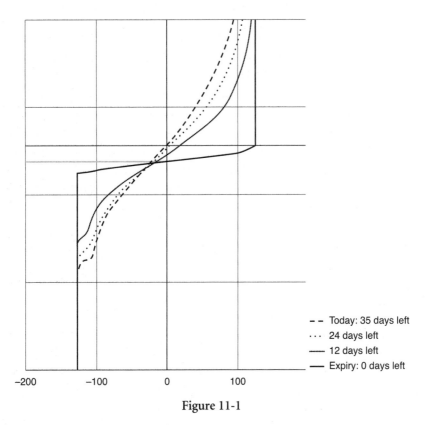

- - Today: 35 days left
- ⋯ 24 days left
- —— 12 days left
- — Expiry: 0 days left

−200   −100   0   100

Figure 11-1

A good goal on these credit spreads is to receive a credit that nearly equals or possibly even exceeds the max risk. This kind of opportunity often presents itself following a special event that produces a dramatic price move accompanied by high volume. Such circumstances often pump the extra premium into the at-the-money options that creates good credit spreads.

As with most credit spreads, time is your friend, which suggests the use of near-term options. In this case with RMBS, the February options were expiring in only eight days, which was a little too soon and did not offer the desired credit. Hence the choice of the March puts for the trade. To realize the max profit on this trade, RMBS just needed to close above $25 at the March options expiration in five weeks.

On March 19, 2004, RMBS closed at $27.21, and the options expired worthless. The maximum profit was realized.

- **Example 2.** Walt Disney Co. (DIS). On February 11, 2004, there was news of the intention of Comcast Corp to buy DIS. The price of DIS rose quickly from the $24 level to a high of $28 on huge volume. It was immediately made clear that DIS regarded this as a hostile offer that would be resisted. So, unless Comcast was going to increase their offer, this situation would be in doubt for the immediate future. Within two days, the excitement was quieting, and the price of DIS began to retreat back to $27. This was a good opportunity to initiate the following credit spread:

Trade: Buy 1 Mar 30 call and sell 1 Mar 27.5 call for a net credit of $1.30 per share.

Credit = $130.

Max risk = $120 [(30.0 − 27.5 − 1.3) × 100 = 120].

See Figure 11-2 for a risk graph that depicts this trade.

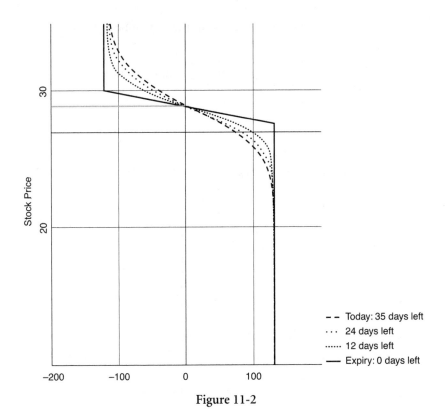

Figure 11-2

In this example, a special event has created considerable
interest in an otherwise quiet stock. The gap up in price on
huge volume pumped extra premium into the at-the-money
options. To achieve a max profit on this credit spread only
required that DIS close below $27.50 at the March options
expiration.

On March 19, 2004, DIS closed at $25.39, and the options
expired worthless. The maximum profit was realized.

■ **Example 3.** Apple Computer Inc. (AAPL). On April 14, 2005,
the stock began to fall from the $40 level with high volume
in spite of a good earnings report. Over the next few
sessions, the stock price fell to $34 before beginning to stabilize.

This was a good opportunity to initiate the following credit spread:

Trade: Buy 1 May 32.5 put and sell 1 May 35 put for a net credit of $1.20 per share.

Credit = $120.

Max risk = $130 [(35 − 32.5 − 1.20) × 100 = 130].

See Figure 11-3 for a risk graph that depicts this trade.

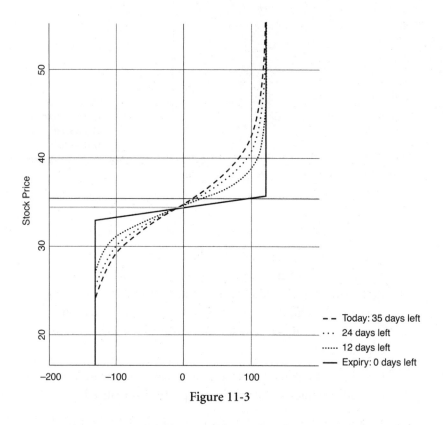

Figure 11-3

In this example, a strong company sold off on good earnings, apparently because investors worried about how long it could continue to produce such outstanding growth. The excessive selling pumped extra premium into the near-term options.

To achieve a max profit on this credit spread only requires that AAPL close above $35 at the May options expiration.

On May 20, 2005, AAPL closed at $37.55, and the options expired worthless. The maximum profit was realized.

Comments

Finding opportunities for these credit spreads does not require hearing about the special event as it is happening. In fact, you should wait a day or two (perhaps even longer) for the price burst associated with the public awareness of the event to exhaust itself. On the other hand, you cannot wait too long, because the extra premium pumped into the option prices will soon dissipate.

It is important to research the background of the special event that caused the dramatic move in the stock price. Make sure it is the type of event that is unlikely to have further repercussions in the near future. The event can be either a good-news or a bad-news situation, as long as it is all of the story. Avoid events announced as "accounting irregularities" or "possible restatement of earnings," because these are all too often followed by further revelations that push the stock down even more.

12

CALENDAR SPREADS

The focus of this chapter is on calendar spread trades, also known as *horizontal spread trades* or *time spread trades.* These trades work best on stocks whose price moves within a reasonably narrow range. Volatile stocks that can move up or down 15 percent within the time frame of one month are generally not suitable for calendar spreads.

In a basic calendar spread, you buy a distant month option and sell a closer month option. Both options have the same strike price, which is typically selected to be the one nearest the price of the stock at the time the trade is initiated. When things progress well in a calendar spread, the short option ultimately expires worthless while the stock price remains essentially unchanged. This leaves the long option with a reduced cost basis, which can be either sold for profit or used for further trading.

Calendar spreads can be created with either call options or with put options. For purposes of this introductory discussion, we assume that call options are used. A comment on using put options for a calendar spread will be included at the end.

Suppose that XYZ has traded in a relatively narrow price range over the past few months and you expect that trend to continue. In early May, XYZ is trading at $34.70, which makes the $35 strike price a good choice for a calendar spread. Here is a typical calendar spread trade on XYZ:

> Trade: Buy 1 Nov 35 call for $3.50 per share and sell 1 Jun 35 call for $1.30 per share.
>
> Cost = $220.
>
> Maximum risk = $220.

See Figure 12-1 for a risk graph that depicts this trade.

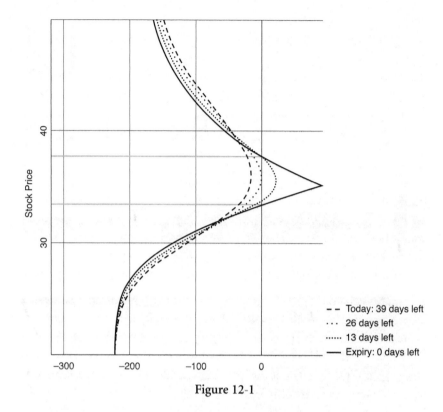

Figure 12-1

Suppose that six weeks later, at the June options expiration date, XYZ is still at $34.70. The short Jun 35 call will expire worthless. This leaves the Nov 35 call with a cost basis of $2.20 per share. Using an options calculator, we can estimate the value of the Nov 35 call at that time to be $3 per share. If on the Monday after the June expiration date, the Nov 35 is sold for that price, then a profit of $80 is achieved [(3.00 – 2.20) × 100 = 80]. That gain is also seen in the risk graph of Figure 12-1. The profit here represents a gain of 36 percent based on the original risk of $220. Note that this gain is achieved in about six weeks.

To understand how this profit was made, let's look at the details of the trade. The Jun 35 call was sold for $1.20 per share, which was all time value. Because the price of XYZ was under $35 at the expiration date, the Jun 35 call expired worthless, and all of that time value is gained. The Nov 35 call lost only $.50 of time value as its price decreased from

$3.50 per share to $3 per share at the June expiration. Our profit was derived from the fact that the November option was less sensitive to the loss of time value than was the June option. Thus, the calendar spread profited by gaining $1.30 per share from the Jun 35 call, while losing only $.50 per share in the Nov 35 call. This resulted in a net profit of $.80 per share [1.30 − .50 = .80].

As an alternative to selling the Nov 35 call following the June expiration date, it may be worthwhile to hold this option and establish a new calendar spread by selling the Jul 35 call. This illustrates one of the potential benefits of calendar spreads, namely the ability to continue selling front-month options to reduce the cost basis of the longer-term option. Let's examine this new calendar spread.

Following the expiration of the Jun 35 call, you are holding one Nov 35 call with an effective cost basis of $2.20 per share. Then sell one Jul 35 call for $1 per share. (Note that this is less than received for the Jun 35 call because there would be only about four weeks until the July expiration date.) Now, your current net debit and maximum risk is $120 [(2.20 − 1.00) × 100 = 120].

At the July expiration date, suppose that XYZ is again at the same price of $34.70. The short Jul 35 call would expire worthless. This leaves the Nov 35 call with an even lower cost basis of $1.20 per share. Using an options calculator, we can estimate the value of the Nov 35 call to be $2 per share. If on the Monday after the July expiration date, the Nov 35 call is sold for that price, a profit of $80 is achieved. That represents a gain of 67 percent based on the current risk of $120.

The preceding results assume a highly idealized scenario in which the price of XYZ at the June expiration date is $34.70, exactly the same as when the trade was initiated in early May. Furthermore, if the trade was continued by selling the Jul 35 call, the stock price was assumed to be again at $34.70 at the July expiration. To have a more realistic view of calendar spreads, we need to see what happens when the stock price is not the same at expiration as it was when the trade was initiated.

Suppose that the price of XYZ has fallen to $33.75 at the June expiration date. The short Jun 35 call will again expire worthless. An options calculator estimates that the value of the Nov 35 call at that time would be $2.50 per share. Selling the Nov 35 call at that value returns a $30 profit [(2.50 − 2.20) × 100 = 30]. Even though the price of XYZ has fallen, there is still a gain on the trade of 9 percent based on the original risk of $220. The lower return in this scenario is a result of not only the lost time value in the Nov 35 call, but also lost intrinsic value due to the lower stock price.

How low can the price of XYZ be at the June expiration and still achieve a profit? An options calculator shows that the break-even point is a stock price of about $33, as seen in Figure 12-1. If the stock price is below that level at the June expiration date, the calendar spread will show a net loss. For example, if XYZ is at $31, the net loss will be about $80. The maximum that can be lost is the original cost of $220 to establish the spread. A loss close to the maximum is incurred if XYZ drops to $25 or less.

Even if XYZ is below $33 at the June expiration and the spread fails to show a profit at that time, it might still be worthwhile to continue holding the Nov 35 call with a reduced cost basis of $2.20 per share. This makes it easier to achieve profitability if the stock price eventually begins to rise.

Consider another scenario in which the price of XYZ has risen to $36.50 at the June expiration date. Then, the short Jun 35 call will have a value of $1.50 per share (all intrinsic value). An options calculator estimates the value of the Nov 35 call to be $4 per share. To close the trade near the June expiration, it is necessary to buy back the Jun 35 call and sell the Nov 35 call for a net of $2.50 per share [4.00 − 1.50 = 2.50]. This represents a profit of $30 [(2.50 − 2.20) × 100 = 30], for a 14 percent gain on the original risk of $220.

In this scenario where XYZ is above $35 at the June expiration, the fact that the Jun 35 call did not expire worthless was offset by the increased value of the Nov 35 call. With an even higher price of XYZ at expiration, the value of the Nov 35 call would also be even higher, but that gain would be offset by an increased value of the Jun 35 call.

How high can the price of XYZ be at the June expiration and still have the calendar spread achieve a profit? An options calculator shows that the break-even point is a stock price of about $38, as seen in Figure 12-1.

At that level, the Jun 35 call would have a value of $3 per share, while the Nov 35 call would have a value of $5.20 per share. Closing out both options would produce $220 [(5.20 − 3.00) × 100 = 220], which exactly offsets the original cost of the spread trade. If the price of XYZ is above $38 at expiration, the price of the Jun 25 call will have increased more than the Nov 35 call. This results in a net difference of less than $220 and hence a loss on the trade. If XYZ reaches $42, the calendar spread will show a net loss of about $100 at expiration.

The Rollout Maneuver

As previously mentioned, a primary feature of the calendar spread is the ability to continue establishing a new calendar spread each month. In the ideal scenario, as illustrated previously, the front-month option is allowed to expire worthless, thereby leaving the long-term option with a reduced cost basis. Then the next-month option with the same strike can be sold to establish the new calendar spread.

The process of converting the old calendar spread into a new calendar spread does not necessarily require waiting until the expiration date arrives. Frequently, the conversion is best accomplished by buying back the front-month option before expiration while simultaneously selling the next-month option. This maneuver is called the *rollout*.

The rollout maneuver is a necessity when the short option is in-the-money as expiration nears. In this situation, the short option must be bought back to avoid an assignment. It may also be advantageous to use a rollout even when the short option is out-of-the-money. What are the circumstances under which a rollout should be considered?

Let's first look at the case where the short option is in-the-money as expiration nears. An in-the-money option will often have lost almost all of its time value with 8 to 10 days still remaining until expiration. In this circumstance, there is a good reason to proceed immediately with a roll into the next month. There is little to be gained from holding the front-month option until expiration, while the next-month option that you hope to sell is undergoing some significant price erosion. The goal is to perform the rollout when the differential between the front-month option and the next-month option is maximized. This frequently occurs before the expiration date.

The case in which the short option is out-of-the-money is a bit different. The market makers will often keep the ask price for an out-of-the-money option abnormally high, even going into the day of expiration. They may keep the ask price at $0.15 per share or higher with only a few days remaining until expiration, so as to make it expensive for you to eliminate the risk of your short option. In this circumstance, it is often best to proceed with the rollout several days early and not wait until expiration just to collect that extra $0.15 per share. Here again, the goal is to perform the rollout when the differential between the front-month option and the next-month option is greatest.

Comments

The objective of a calendar spread trade is to capture the time value in a front-month option, which will decay faster than the time value in a more distant month option. To exploit this difference, it is generally wise to initially have at least one month between the expiration of the long option and that of the short option. This allows for at least one new calendar spread to be established after the first expiration date.

A calendar spread is only profitable if the stock price at the options expiration date is within a fairly narrow range. The risk graph of Figure 12-1 is fairly typical for a calendar spread. As seen in that example, the range of profitability at the June expiration was $33 to $38. This means that the price of XYZ at expiration needs to be within a price range that is neither 9 percent above nor 6 percent below the $35 strike price to achieve a profit. This emphasizes the importance of analyzing the expected trading range of a stock being considered for a calendar spread.

The preceding discussion focused on calendar spread trades using call options. Calendar spread trades using put options can work equally well. Often the decision as to whether to use calls or puts for a calendar spread depends upon a more likely direction of drift in the stock price. Generally speaking, a call spread is used when the expected drift is toward a higher stock price, whereas a put spread is used when a downward drift in the stock price is considered more likely.

When should a calendar spread be abandoned? Although it is true that you can never lose more than your original debit in a calendar spread trade, it may nevertheless be prudent to exit early to limit your loss. A reasonable criterion is to exit a calendar spread when the loss reaches 50 percent of the amount paid to establish the trade.

When should you take a profit and terminate the calendar spread rather than establish a new calendar in the next month? Anytime you can realize at least 50 percent of the maximum possible profit in a calendar spread, consider closing the trade for a profit.

13*

ADVANCED CALENDAR SPREADS

his chapter discuses some advanced concepts for calendar spreads.

Volatility Skew Trades

Implied volatility (IV) is one of the most important pieces of options data used in finding a good calendar spread. The primary use of IV is to determine whether an option is comparatively overpriced or under-priced. Most options friendly brokerage firms provide IV data for options. The value of the IV for an option is calculated from a theoretical model for options pricing known as the *Black-Scholes formula*. Some discussion of the calculation of implied volatility is provided in Chapter 29, "Implied Volatility and the Black-Scholes Formula."

If the current IV of an option is high compared to an annual average, it means that the price of the option is inflated with extra time value. In the case of calendar spreads, the IV data is used to make a comparison between the long and short legs of the spread. To increase our chance for success with a calendar spread, we want the short leg of the spread to be overpriced as compared with the long leg. This *volatility skew* is observed when the IV of the short option is larger than the IV of the long option.

The numeric value of the volatility skew is the percentage increase in the IV of the short option as compared with the IV of the long option. You might think that the greater the skew, the better the chance for a successful calendar spread. Unfortunately, this is not necessarily true. Typically, volatility skews between 10 percent and 25 percent work best. Be suspicious of IV skews that are 30 percent or greater, particularly when both options have unusually high IVs.

An unusually high volatility skew often means that the front-month options are being used for wild speculation in the underlying stock due to some impending event that could dramatically alter the stock price. For example, prior to an announcement of FDA approval (or disapproval) of a drug, it is common to observe IV skews of 50 percent and greater. The danger here for a calendar spread is twofold: (1) When the event happens, it may instantaneously move the stock price out of the profitability range of the calendar spread. (2) Even if the stock price remains unchanged, all the volatility will quickly collapse back to more normal levels after the event has passed. This IV collapse is called a *volatility crush*. Because this crush affects all the options, the price of the long option in the calendar spread will be crushed to a fraction of its original value, thereby destroying the potential for a profit in the trade.

The bottom line here is that we want a "Goldilocks" IV skew: not too cold and not too hot, but just right.

Let's look at some examples of calendar spreads with a reasonable volatility skew:

- **Example 1.** In early May, XYZ is trading at $16.90, which makes the $17.50 strike price a reasonable choice for a call calendar spread. The IV for the Jun 17.5 call is 49, whereas the IV for the Jan 17.5 call is only 41. That gives a skew of 19.5 percent [(49 − 41)/41 = 0.195].

  Trade 1: Buy 1 Jan (05) 17.5 call for $2.10 per share and sell 1 Jun 17.5 call for $1.15 per share. The net debit and maximum risk on this trade is $95 [(2.10 − 1.15) × 100 = 95].

See Figure 13-1 for a risk graph that depicts this trade.

This risk graph shows that the range of profitability is between $15 and $23. A maximum profit of $125 for a gain of 132 percent occurs if

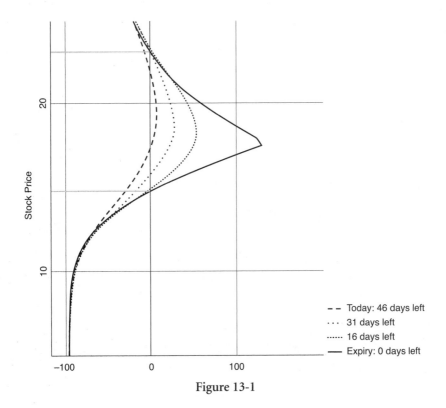

Figure 13-1

XYZ closes at exactly $17.50 at the June options expiration. If XYZ closes between $16 and $20.50, the spread should show a profit between $50 and $125, for a gain between 53 percent and the maximum of 132 percent.

For a comparison, let's look at a calendar spread on XYZ that uses put options. With XYZ trading at $16.90, the $15 strike price seems like a reasonable choice for a put calendar spread.

> Trade 2: Buy 1 Jan 15 put for $1.60 per share and sell 1 Jun 15 put for $.80 per share. Then, net debit and maximum risk on this trade is $80 [(1.60 − .80) × 100 = 80].

The IV for the Jan (05) 15 put is 44, whereas the IV for the Jun 15 put is 52. That gives a skew of 18.2 percent [(52 − 44)/44 = 0.182].

See Figure 13-2 for a risk graph that depicts this trade.

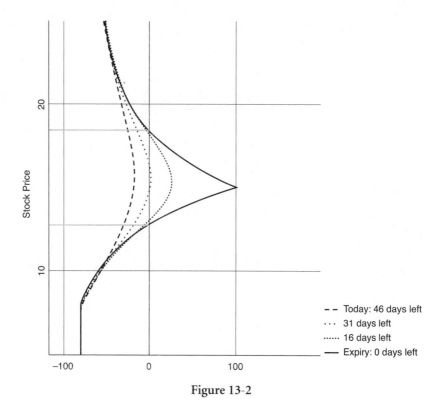

Figure 13-2

This risk graph shows that the range of profitability is between $13 and $18. A maximum profit of $100, for a gain of 125 percent, occurs if XYZ closes at exactly $15 at the June options expiration. If XYZ closes between $13.50 and $17, the spread should show a profit between $30 and $100, for a gain between 38 percent and the maximum of 125 percent.

Comments

Always do a little research on the stock you are considering for a calendar spread. You want to determine whether there is any upcoming company event that might affect the IV of its options.

In comparing the call calendar spread (Trade 1) with the put calendar spread (Trade 2), we note that the call spread is shifted toward a higher price range, whereas the put spread is shifted toward a lower price range. This is typical of slightly out-of-the-money calendar spreads because the maximum gain always occurs at the strike price.

The call spread and the put spread had about the same volatility skew, but the call spread had a wider range of profitability ($15 to $23 for the call spread versus $13 to $18 for the put spread). Part of the reason for this was that the $17.50 strike used for the calls was closer to the stock price of $16.90 than was the $15 strike price used for the puts.

If we had used in-the-money options instead of slightly out-of-the-money options for these calendar spreads, the range of profitability would have been a little narrower, whereas the maximum gain at the strike price would have been larger. The reason for the larger gain is that the option being sold has intrinsic value as well as time value. Then, as the stock price moves toward the strike price, both intrinsic value and time value are being captured. Of course, the long option is also losing intrinsic value, but its overall price may be less affected. The bottom line here is that if there is any benefit from using in-the-money options for a calendar spread, it must be determined on an individual case basis.

Ratio Calendar Spread Trades

A useful modification of the classic calendar spread trade is the ratio calendar spread trade. The ratio concept simply means that fewer contracts are sold than are bought. The purpose of having more long contacts than short ones is to remove the constraint on one end of the profitability range, thereby allowing for unlimited profit if the stock price makes a large move in the appropriate direction.

Using either call or put options for the ratio calendar spread, fewer near month contracts are sold than the number purchased of distant month contacts. With calls, this has the effect of opening the upper end of the risk graph for unlimited profit if the stock price moves higher. Analogously, with puts, this has the effect of opening the lower end of the risk graph for unlimited profit if the stock price moves lower.

The key issue here is what should be the ratio of long contracts to short contracts to achieve the best return. On the one hand, we want to keep the cost basis low by having almost as many short options as long ones. On the other hand, we want to achieve an increasing profit level if the stock moves in the appropriate direction. Although there is no unique answer here, some experience shows that ratios such as 3:2 or 4:3 are good ones to consider.

To illustrate a ratio call calendar spread, let's modify the above Trade 1 with a 4:3 ratio.

> Trade 3: Buy 4 Jan (05) 17.5 calls for $2.10 per share and sell 3 Jun 17.5 calls for $1.15 per share. The net debit and maximum risk on this trade is $495 [(2.10 × 400) − (1.15 × 300) = 495].

See Figure 13-3 for a risk graph that depicts this trade.

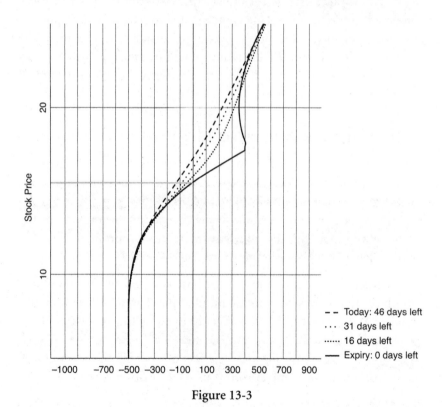

Figure 13-3

It is seen that the range of profitability at expiration is any price above $15.60. In comparison with Trade 1, the lower bound of the profitability range has been raised only slightly, whereas the upper bound has been entirely removed.

For the standard calendar spread of Trade 1, the maximum return was achieved only if XYZ closed at exactly the strike price of $17.50 at the June expiration. Although the maximum return on investment was 132 percent, that figure dropped off quickly if the closing price deviated up or down from $17.50. By comparison, the ratio calendar spread of Trade 3 has a return on investment of 81 percent at the strike price $17.50, but has the benefit that the return is essentially the same for any stock price up to $21. Above $21, things get even better as the return rapidly increases without limit.

Comments

If you want to allow for a possible move in the stock price that would take it outside of the range of profitability, consider modifying the standard calendar spread to that of a ratio calendar spread. As a starting point, look at the number of long contracts versus the number of short contracts in ratios of 3:2 or 4:3.

Deep-in-the-Money LEAPS Put Calendar Spreads

This is a special type of calendar spread intended for a 9 to 12-month bullish position on stocks that have LEAPS put options. These trades provide high leverage, but may require some unusual maintenance. To do this type of trade, the stock must offer LEAPS puts with strike prices well above the current stock price. It helps if those puts also have significant open interest, although you may be able to work around that issue if necessary.

Basic strategy: Buy one long-term LEAPS put (21 to 24 months until expiration) with a strike price that is well above the current price of the stock and sell one nearer-term LEAPS put (9 to 12 months until expiration) with the same strike price.

This creates a calendar spread where both legs are deep-in-the-money puts.

The important feature of these deep-in-the-money puts is that they will have relatively little time value included in their prices. Thus, even though the long and short options are a year apart in expiration dates, they will have nearly the same price. This will make the cost of this calendar spread quite low and hence offer substantial leverage.

In the scenario for maximum profit on this spread, the stock will rise over time so as to reach the strike price of the options at the expiration date of the short leg. With the short put expiring worthless, the long put will still have one full year's worth of value, which can be immediately sold to achieve maximum profit.

The maintenance issue on this type of spread arises if you receive an assignment on the short option. Typically, this only occurs if all the time value disappears and the open interest is quite low. The remedy is to sell the stock assigned to you and resell the same put option simultaneously. Be sure to do these two transactions together so as to reestablish the spread at no net cost (aside from trade commissions). That is, make sure that the proceeds received from the reselling the put option will match the difference between the prices at which you buy and sell the stock.

To illustrate this deep-in-the-money LEAPS put calendar spread, consider ZYX stock with a current price of $49. You expect ZYX to be at $65 in nine months.

> Trade 4: Buy 1 Jan (08) 65 put at $19.30 per share and sell 1 Jan (07) 65 put at $17.90 per share for a net debit of $1.40 per share.
>
> Cost = $140.
>
> Max risk = $140.

See Figure 13-4 for a risk graph that depicts this trade.

Note that although the options being bought and sold are individually quite expensive, the net cost for establishing the spread is only $140.

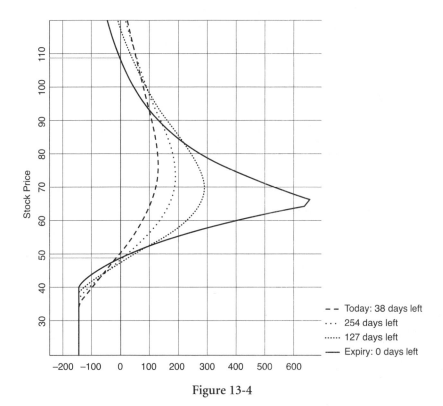

Figure 13-4

The maximum profit occurs when ZYX stock is at $65 as the Jan (07) put expires worthless. An option calculator indicates the long Jan (08) 65 put would have a price of $8.20 per share. That represents a profit of $680 [820 − 140 = 680], as seen in Figure 13-4, for a gain of 485 percent. If the price of ZYX is in the range of $57 to $77, the profit would be at least $310, for a gain of 225 percent or better. The downside break-even point is ZYX at $49 at expiration.

Diagonal Calendar Spread Trades

Another version of the calendar spread is the *diagonal spread*, which uses a different strike price in the front-month option than in the back month. The basic idea is to select the long option to have a strike price that is out-of-the-money compared to the strike price of the short option. This reduces the cost of the calendar and in some cases even creates an initial credit.

The diagonal spread trade frequently works best when the two strike prices are no more than $2.50 apart, because it keeps the maximum risk on the trade at a reasonable level. This means restricting this type of trade to either low-priced or some medium-priced stocks, as well as various indexes that have closely spaced strike prices.

Let's look at an example involving the S&P 500 index as represented by the SPDRs Trust (SPY), which has strike prices separated by $1. The SPY is currently trading at $124.

> Trade: Buy 1 Oct 126 call and sell 1 Sept 124 call for a net credit of $.25 per share.
>
> Initial Credit = $25.
>
> Max risk = $175.

See Figure 13-5 for a risk graph that depicts this trade.

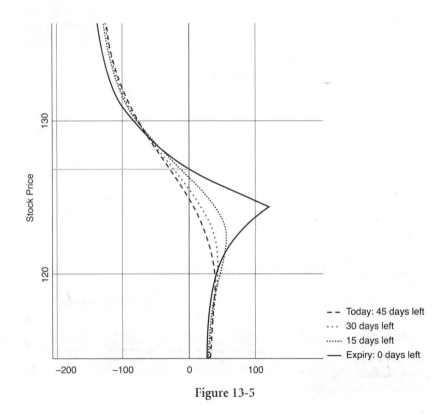

Figure 13-5

The risk graph in Figure 13-5 is typical of a diagonal spread with call options, which is done for an initial credit. The risk graph calculator estimates a break-even price of $126.25 at the September options expiration date. Any price of the SPY below that level leads to a profit. If the SPY price falls to a low level, the profit is the initial credit received on the trade. To suffer the maximum loss requires the SPY price to rise to an extremely high level. In practice, the risk would be significantly less than the theoretical maximum of $175.

An alternate view of the diagonal spread trade is the combination of a regular calendar spread and a front-month credit spread. In the case of the preceding example trade, consider the following two trades:

Calendar spread: Buy 1 Oct 126 call and sell 1 Sept 126 call for a net debit of $.30 per share.

Vertical spread: Buy 1 Sept 126 call and sell 1 Sept 124 call for a net credit of $.55 per share.

When both of these trades are done together, the sale of the Sept 124 call in the calendar spread is cancelled by the purchase of the same option in the vertical spread. The result of this cancellation is the diagonal spread trade shown in Figure 13-5. In essence, the vertical spread provides a credit that finances the cost of the calendar spread.

The diagonal spread offers several alternatives at the expiration date of the front-month option. In the SPY trade shown above, if the price of the SPY is below $124 at the September options expiration date, the short call will expire worthless. This leaves the Oct 126 call free to become part of another trade. For example, a bear call spread could be created by selling Oct 124 call.

When the diagonal spread is created with calls, the attitude is that the price of the underlying stock or index will move either sideways or downward. As seen in Figure 13-5, the profit zone caters to a sideways or downward movement of the SPY price. When the diagonal spread is done with puts, the profit zone caters to a sideways or upward movement.

14

COVERED CALLS

One of the first strategies that someone new to options hears about is the *covered call trade.* Frequently, this strategy is touted as a safe and simple way to make money with options. Many brokerage firms allow covered calls as the only option trade that can be made in a retirement account because it is "conservative."

Unfortunately, describing covered call trades as conservative is somewhat misleading. Those same brokers who only allow covered call trades in retirement accounts will claim that selling naked puts is much too risky to be allowed in a retirement account. Well, at least they got that part correct—selling naked puts does involve significant risk. The truth is that a covered call trade carries essentially the same risk as selling a naked put. Later, it will demonstrated why this is true.

In its simplest form, the covered call trade requires that you own 100 shares of stock and then sell 1 out-of-the-money call contract. In this trade, the short call is described as *covered* because it is secured by your long stock. If the option is exercised, you possess the stock required for sale at the strike price.

The cash received from selling the call is yours to keep, provided that you do not decide later to buy back the call. If the stock price is above the strike price of the call at expiration, your stock will be called away for a price that is higher than it was when you sold the call. Thus, you have made money on the stock as well as the option. On the other hand, if the stock price is below the strike price of the call at expiration, the option expires worthless and you keep your stock. Then, the money received from the sale of the option has reduced the cost basis of your stock, and you are free to repeat the process in the next monthly option cycle.

If the covered call trade can be successfully repeated month after month, it has the potential to produce a regular infusion of cash into your brokerage account. Unfortunately, the process is not as simple as it might seem. To do covered call trading, you need to understand the inherent risk in this type of trade and be prepared to make some tough decisions as each month's expiration date draws near.

An Idealized Trade

Let's first examine how an idealized covered call trade might work to perfection.

You buy 100 shares of XYZ at $30 per share for a total investment of $3,000. Over the next seven months, this stock averages a monthly rise of 9.5 percent as it moves up to $50 per share, for a great $2,000 profit. To enhance this profit in each month along the way, you sell 1 call contract (1 contract = 100 shares) on XYZ at a strike price that is about 10 percent to 15 percent above the stock price. Suppose that your selling price for each covered call is $1.20 per share, which brings in an additional $120 per month. Assuming that the price of XYZ is never above the strike price of the current month option as it expires, you will be able to hold the stock through all seven months while bringing in an additional profit of $840 [7 × 120 = 840]. So, when this covered call strategy is working perfectly, you have increased your profit on this investment from $2,000 (67 percent) to $2,840 (95 percent).

Although this idealized scenario could happen as described, it rarely does. The most unrealistic aspect of this idealized trade is that it requires the stock price to move up month by month in a perfectly coordinated manner with the strike price of the short call.

A Realistic Trade

Let's look at a real-life example of a covered call trade that did not progress quite so idealistically.

In the preceding idealized example, the overall price movement of XYZ is similar to that of Qualcomm Inc (QCOM) during 2003. From May 2003 to December 2003, QCOM moved from $30 to $50. Unfortunately, the month-by-month price movement of QCOM was not always coordinated with the options expiration date so as to allow for an easy decision about how to proceed into the next month.

Suppose that you bought 100 shares of QCOM in May 2003 for $30 and sold 1 Jun 35 call for $1 a share. See Figure 14-1 for the risk graph that depicts this trade. Note in the risk graph that the maximum profit on the trade is $600 no matter how high the stock price climbs.

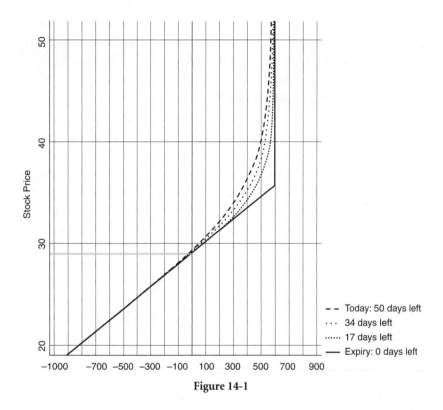

Figure 14-1

When the June expiration date arrives, you are confronted with a difficult decision, because the stock price is near $37. Do you (1) buy back the short option for a loss so as to continue holding the stock or (2) do you give up on any future gains in the stock by letting it be called away, for a quick profit of $6 per share [35 − 30 + 1 = 6]?

If you decide to hold on to the stock, you must buy back the short call for $2 per share, resulting in a loss of $1 per share in the option. You could then sell the Jul 40 call for $2 per share. At the July expiration, the $40 call expired worthless because QCOM had fallen back to $35. You again had a difficult decision to make. Do you (1) sell one Aug 40 call for only $.35 per share, while hoping for the stock price to recover, or (2) sell one Aug 35 call for $2 per share in case the stock continues to fall or just goes sideways for the next month?

So, in both of the first two months of this trade, tough decisions had to be made. In later months, other difficult decisions presented themselves. Although not every month will necessarily pose such problems, you can be sure that similar difficult decisions are going to arise if you plan to hold your stock over a long period of time. The lesson here is that the actual management of covered calls is rarely as straightforward as described by an idealized example.

Covered Call vs. Naked Put

Now let's get back to the issue of the risk in a covered call trade. To make things definite, we will again use QCOM as an example. In late December 2003, you buy 100 shares of QCOM at $53, and to complete the covered call trade, you sell 1 Feb 55 call for $2 per share. This means that you have equivalently purchased the stock for $51 per share, and hence your maximum risk on this covered call trade is $5,100. See Figure 14-2 for a risk graph that depicts this trade.

If QCOM is above $55 at the February options expiration, your stock will be called away, which provides you a profit of $4 per share [55 − 51 = 4]. On the other hand, if QCOM has fallen to $45 as the option expires, you will be able to keep your stock, but the value of your stock will have decreased by $6 per share [51 − 45 = 6]. Now you are showing a loss of $600 on the covered call trade.

Let's compare this "conservative" covered call trade with the "risky" trade of selling a naked put on QCOM. Instead of buying QCOM stock, suppose that you sell one Feb 55 put for $4 per share. The risk here is that you will be required to buy 100 shares of QCOM at the equivalent price of $51 per share [55 − 4 = 51], so again your maximum risk is $5,100. See Figure 14-3 for a risk graph that depicts this trade.

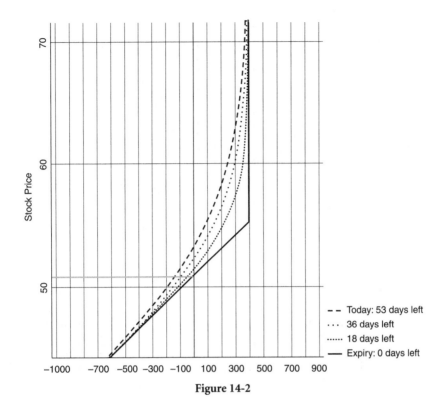

Figure 14-2

If QCOM is above $55 at the February options expiration, the short option will expire worthless and the cash brought in from selling the put can then be counted as a $4 profit $[4 - 0 = 4]$. On the other hand, if QCOM has fallen to $45 as the option expires, the put will be exercised, requiring you to buy the stock at $55 per share. This means that you will then own 100 shares of QCOM stock in which you have suffered a loss of $6 per share $[55 - 4 - 45 = 6]$.

Thus, in either trade, similar circumstances lead to the same result of net profit or net loss. This equivalence of the two trades is further demonstrated by comparing Figure 14-2 with Figure 14-3. The bottom line is that no matter what QCOM does, our profit or loss in selling a naked put is the same as the covered call trade.

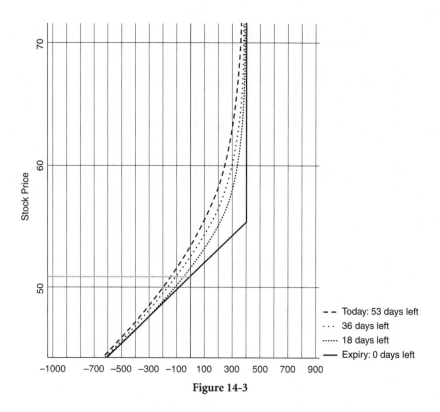

Figure 14-3

Comments

Covered call trades are not really "conservative." Buying 100 shares of stock typically involves a significant outlay of capital. If the stock price then falls precipitously, the dollar loss on the trade can be substantial. This loss is exactly the same as if a naked put was sold and then the stock price fell. Also, the potential profit from a covered call is capped, just as it is when a naked put is sold.

The month-by-month management of covered call trades can be tricky. Some months are going to require a tough decision as the expiration date arrives.

One advantage enjoyed by a covered call over a naked put is that you do participate in any dividend payments. Naked put positions enjoy the advantage of tying up less cash and creating extra leverage in your brokerage account. You must, however, be wary of using that extra leverage in an unwise manner, such as increasing the size of your naked put position beyond a reasonable level. This can lead to an unpleasant margin call from your broker if the stock suffers a sudden drop.

Here are some suggestions for handling covered call trades:

1. Because almost all your risk is in what you paid for the stock, keep you eyes on the stock price and to a much lesser extent on the option price. Decide on an appropriate stop loss price for the stock, and if it falls to that level, protect the major portion of your investment by selling the stock and buying back the call. Do not hang on to a falling stock to collect an extra $.40 on the short option.

2. When deciding on the strike price of the call that you are going to sell, make sure it is a price you will feel comfortable about giving up your stock if that becomes necessary. If your primary goal is to keep your stock, select a higher strike price. If you are willing to sell your stock at a price closer to its current value, pick a nearby strike price to bring in more cash.

3. Do not go too far out in time. Those juicy premiums in the longer-term options are tempting, but you will generally do better by selling either the front-month call or the next month out. In today's volatile market, the price of a stock can move significantly (up or down) in four to eight weeks. By selling near-month options, you will be better placed to make an adjustment when the expiration date arrives.

4. Do not be greedy. If the stock price is above the strike price at expiration, avoid buying back the option for a loss unless you have a good reason to do so. If you have followed Step 2, you should be willing to let the stock go and take your profit. Avoid the situation in which you buy back the option for a loss to keep your stock, and then have the stock price collapse. This compounds a loss on the option with a loss on the stock.

15

STRADDLES AND STRANGLES

The *straddle trade* and the *strangle trade* are intended to take advantage of stock movement in either direction. They use a combination of a call option and a put option to benefit from a significant move up or down in the stock price.

The Straddle Trade

Upon first learning about the straddle trade, it sounds like the answer to a trader's dream. You will hear that, with a straddle, you do not need to guess which way the stock will move. The straddle can make money if either the stock price goes up or it goes down. What could be better than that?

The basic idea of a straddle trade is to buy a call and buy a put with the same strike price. These options should also have the same expiration month, usually about two to three months in the future. The reason given for doing this type of trade is that if the stock price goes up, the call will show a profit; and if the stock price goes down, the put will show a profit. The catch here is that when one option shows a profit, the other option will show a loss.

Even though the straddle trade concept sounds wonderful, it is actually one of the more difficult option trades with which to make a profit. For the straddle to become profitable, the stock price must move far enough so that the profit in one option more than offsets the loss in the other. If the stock price manages only a modest move in either direction before the options expire, the trade will lose money.

The major obstacle to a successful straddle trade is time. Remember that when you own an option, time is your enemy. With a straddle, you own two options, so time is working against both legs of the trade.

Sooner or later, you will want to try a straddle trade. Under the right circumstances, a straddle can work well. The difficulty is in identifying a stock that meets the right criteria.

Let's look at an example of a straddle trade:

- **Example 1.** In late May, XYZ stock is trading around $30. There is conflicting news surrounding XYZ. Some reports are saying that the company will soon issue a warning that its next quarter earnings will fall far short of expectations. Other reports are suggesting that a competitor is planning to make an offer to buy out XYZ at a substantial premium.

  To cater to either of these dramatic events, you initiate a straddle trade by buying both a call option and a put option with the same strike price. Here is how that might look:

  Trade: Buy 1 Aug 30 call for $2.10 per share and buy 1 Aug 30 put for $1.90 per share.

  Cost = $400 [(2.10 + 1.90) × 100 = 400].

  Max risk = $400.

Figure 15-1 provides a risk graph that depicts this trade.

Now the argument is made that you do not care what happens with XYZ. If the stock makes a big move up or down, one of your options is going to provide a nice profit. This is the attractive feature of the straddle trade; it has the potential to make money no matter which way the stock moves.

First, let's consider some ideal scenarios which lead to profitable outcomes for this straddle trade on XYZ:

1. In mid-June, the earnings warning on XYZ is issued, and the stock price quickly drops to $25. Because of the rapid drop, the price of the Aug 30 put expands to $6.20 per share. The Aug 30 call still has two months before expiration and manages to hold on to a price of $.50 a share. By selling both options for a total of $670 [(6.20 + .50) × 100 = 670], you have made a $270 profit for a gain of 68 percent.

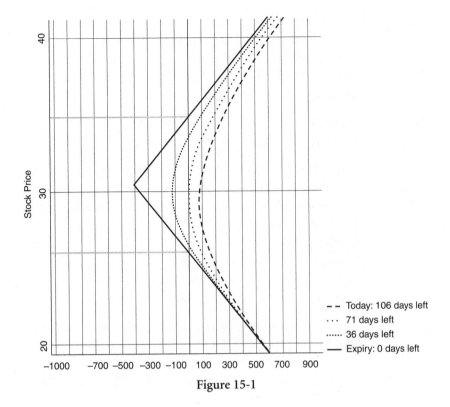

Figure 15-1

2. There is no earnings warning and in early July an offer is made to buy out XYZ at $35 per share. The price of XYZ stock becomes essentially frozen at the buy out price, and the options lose most of their time value. The Aug 30 call is priced at $5.30 per share and the Aug 30 put at $.20 per share. By selling both options for a total of $550 [(5.30 + .20) × 100 = 550], you have made a $150 profit for a gain of 38 percent.

3. Occasionally, it is possible to profit from both options. When XYZ issues the earnings warning that drops the stock to $25, you sell the Aug 30 put for $6.20 per share. The put leg of the straddle has then produced a profit of $430 [(6.20 − 1.90) × 100 = 430]. Having a guaranteed profit of $30 [430 − 400 = 30] on the overall trade, you decide not to sell your Aug 30 call for $.50 per share, but rather hold it for future developments. This decision is rewarded a few weeks later when the deal to buy XYZ at $35 does take place and

you are able to sell the Aug 30 call for $5.30 per share. The call leg of the straddle has then produced a profit $320 [(5.30 − 2.10) × 100 = 320]. The combined profits from both legs of the straddle trade is $750 [430 + 320 = 750], for a fantastic gain of 188 percent.

Now let's be a little more realistic and see how easy it is for the possible outcomes of the straddle trade to be less than ideal:

1A. The disappointing earnings for XYZ are not revealed until late July, and the stock price only drops to $27.50. With just a few weeks remaining until the options expire, there is little time value remaining in the Aug 30 put, which is priced at $2.80 per share. The Aug 30 call is priced at only $.20 per share. You exit both options for $300 [(2.80 + .20) × 100 = 300]. This represents a loss of $100 or 25 percent of your original investment of $400.

2A. There is no earnings warning and in early August a hostile offer for XYZ at $32 is made public. Again with just a couple of weeks of life remaining in the Aug 30 call, it is priced at only $2.30 per share, whereas the Aug 30 put has fallen to $.15 per share. You exit both options for $245 [(2.30 + .15) × 100 = 245]. This represents a loss of $155, or 39 percent of your original investment.

3A. You wait hopefully until the second week of August, but no bad earnings news or potential buyout of XYZ is reported. The stock price has remained in a narrow range around $30 ever since you initiated the straddle trade. Now with almost no time remaining until the options expire, the Aug 30 call is priced at $.80 per share and the Aug 30 put at $.60 per share. If you exit both options for $140 [(.80 + .60) × 100 = 140], you will have experienced a loss of $360, or 90 percent of your original investment.

By contrasting the losing outcomes 1A, 2A, and 3A with the profitable outcomes of 1, 2, and 3, several drawbacks of the straddle trade become apparent. Most important, any event that you are expecting to move the stock price must be significant enough to cause a large increase in the price of the appropriate option. Also, the event must occur relatively soon after initiating the straddle to avoid the loss of too much time value. With a straddle, the ongoing loss of time value is doubly harmful because it is occurring in both options of the trade.

There is another subtle danger with straddle trades. If the rumors about a possible price-altering event are fairly well circulated, the prices of the at-the-money options will become inflated due to the increase in implied volatility (see Chapter 28, "Theory of Maximum Pain"). This makes it more expensive to initiate the straddle, thereby reducing the chance for a profit even if the desired event does come to pass. In the preceding example, a heightened interest in XYZ might increase the purchase price of the Aug 30 call and Aug 30 put by $.85 per share each. Then the cost of initiating the straddle would become $570. Now outcome 2 results in a loss, and 1 is substantially less profitable.

Comments

The key to a successful straddle trade is to identify a stock that satisfies the right criteria. Here are some guidelines:

1. The stock price should be within the range of $20 to $50. If the stock is cheaper than $20, it may not have enough room for the price to fall. If the stock price is above $50, the options may be too expensive to create a straddle with a good potential for profit.

2. Identify an upcoming event that could significantly impact the price of the stock. Ideally, the event needs to be such that the stock price will rise on positive news and fall on negative news. Good candidates are earnings announcements, court decisions, and FDA rulings.

3. The upcoming event should be at least 30 to 60 days away. The options used for the straddle should not expire until at least 30 days after the expected event. This typically means that the options used will have a life of at least 60 to 90 days at the time the straddle is initiated.

4. The upcoming event should not yet have generated enough excitement to cause the options prices to be overly inflated. This can be judged in several ways. Check the level of open

interest and trading volume in the options. Compare the current implied volatility of the options against historical averages.

5. Look for a stock that has been trading sideways within a narrow price range. This signifies an even battle between the buyers and sellers of the stock. When the stock does breakout (up or down), the option prices will gain extra time value and the straddle has an increased potential for profit.

Here are some guidelines for exiting the straddle trade:

1. Sometimes it will be best to exit one side of the straddle before the expected event occurs. For example, in an earnings run, the stock price may move up sharply just prior to the scheduled earnings announcement. In this case, it may be wise to take the profit on the call leg before the actual announcement and hold the put until afterward. If the stock price then falls after the announcement, there will be a better exit price for the put.

2. Do not stay in the straddle too long after the event has taken place. If the event does cause a significant move in the stock price, it will temporarily pump extra time value into the price of the profitable option. Sell the profitable option before that extra time value shrinks.

3. Never hold both sides of the straddle until expiration. Generally, this will lead to a near maximum loss on the trade. If nothing has happened to create a price move, the straddle will lose a substantial portion of its value during the last three to four weeks of its life. Exit when there is at least three to four weeks before the options expire to recover what you can of your original investment. This is the reason that options expiring at least 30 days after the expected event are used in the straddle trade.

The Strangle Trade

A strangle trade is similar to a straddle trade, except that the call and put options have different strike prices. The idea is to lower the cost of the trade by using out-of-the-money options. Essentially, this is a more aggressive version of the straddle trade.

Let's reconsider Example 1, where XYZ is trading around $30 in late May. Now try to play the upcoming events with a strangle trade.

Trade: Buy 1 Aug 35 call for $.80 per share and buy 1 Aug 25 put for $.70 per share.

Cost = $150 [(0.80 + 0.70) × 100 = 150].

Max risk = $150.

See Figure 15-2 for a risk graph that depicts this trade.

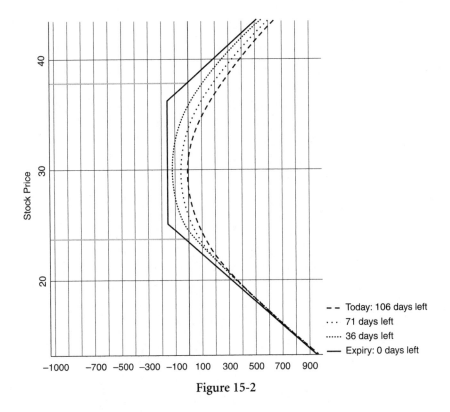

Figure 15-2

This straddle trade is a much cheaper trade than the corresponding straddle trade. A comparison of Figure 15-1 and Figure 15-2 indicates that for the strangle to achieve the same percentage profit after 70 days requires a larger move in the stock price.

16

STOCK REPAIR
AND STOCK
ENHANCEMENT

W e all have experienced the situation in which we buy a good stock only to see it undergo a significant pullback in price. We still like the stock and feel that it will recover at least some of the ground that it lost. There is a low-cost option strategy that can help you get back to a break-even status when the stock regains only part of its lost value. The same strategy also can be used to greatly enhance your profit in a stock for essentially no additional expense beyond the original cost of the stock.

The *stock repair strategy* uses options to assist in bringing your stock investment back to a break-even level. This strategy is structured to attain the break-even status at a stock price that is significantly lower than the original purchase price. The great appeal of this strategy is that it involves no additional risk since it can be applied for little or no additional expense.

Another version of this strategy, referred to as the *stock enhancement strategy*, can be used to greatly improve the return on a stock that you have purchased. As with the stock repair strategy, little or no additional expense is required. The stock enhancement strategy provides even greater leverage when the stock itself is replaced by a cheaper substitute, such as an in-the-money, long-term call with a high delta.

The basic concept is essentially the same for both of these strategies. We discuss that concept and use examples to illustrate the strategies.

Stock Repair Strategy

For this strategy to work, it is necessary for your fallen stock to make at least a partial recovery. The stock repair strategy uses options to expand that partial recovery into a full recovery of your original investment, with little or no additional expense. If the stock price remains unchanged or continues to fall, this strategy offers no help.

The basic plan is to buy one at-the-money call for each 100 shares of stock that you own. You are going to pay for this one long call by selling two out-of-the money calls with the same expiration date. The idea is to use the cash received from the two short calls to pay for the one long call. Choose an expiration month for the options that is far enough out in time for the price of your stock to recover back to the strike price of the short calls.

Let's look at some examples to illustrate the stock repair strategy:

- **Example 1**. You bought 100 shares of XYZ back in December when it was $35. You watched it initially go up, but then undergo a dramatic slide to its current price in early March of $23. You still like the stock and feel that there is some hope for a recovery, although getting back to break-even at $35 seems far away. Let's see how stock repair might help.

   Trade: Buy 1 Jun 25 call for $3.30 per share and sell 2 Jun 30 calls for $1.75 per share. This actually produces a net credit of $.20 per share [(1.75 × 2) − 3.3 = .20].

   Position: Along with an extra $.20 per share in your account, you hold the combination of a covered call (long 100 shares XYZ and short 1 Jun 30 call) and a bull call spread (long 1 Jun 25 call and short 1 Jun 30 call). See Figure. 16-1 for a risk graph that depicts this position.

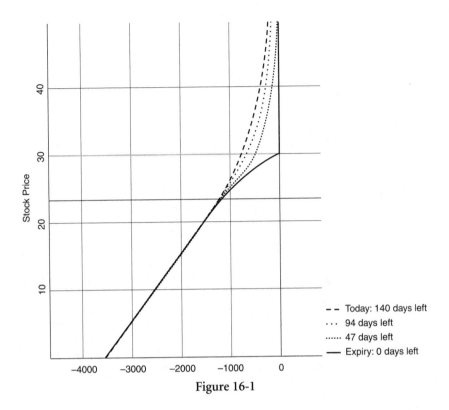

Figure 16-1

Payoff: If XYZ is above $30 at the June options expiration, the stock will be called away at $30 per share, for a $7 per share gain over its present price of $23. The bull call spread will be worth $5 per share. The total gain (including the $.20 credit received) is $12.20 per share [7.0 + 5.0 + .2 = 12.2], which is equivalent to a stock price of $35.20. Thus, you will have reached slightly better than break-even, although the stock is still as much as $5 below your original purchase price.

- **Example 2.** You bought 100 shares of YZX back in December when it was $19.50. Now in early March the stock is down 15 percent with a slide to $16.50. Let's see how stock repair can get you back to slightly better than break-even in only 10 weeks with the stock recovering just 6 percent from its current level.

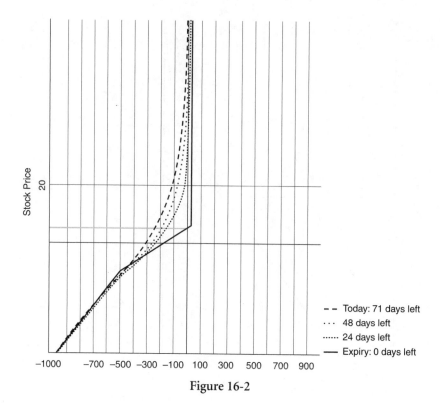

Figure 16-2

Trade: Buy 1 May 15 call for $2.40 per share and sell 2 May 17.5 calls for $1.10 per share. This does require a small cash outlay, specifically $.20 per share [(1.1 × 2) − 2.4 = −.2].

Position: It has cost you an extra $.20 per share to hold the combination of a covered call (long 100 shares of YZX and short 1 May 17.5 call) and a bull call spread (long 1 May 15 call and short 1 May 17.5 call). See Figure. 16-2 for a risk graph that depicts this position.

Payoff: If YZX is up by only 6 percent from its current level to $17.50 at the May options expiration, you will be slightly better than break-even. The stock will be called away at $17.50 per share for a $1 per share gain over its present price of $16.50. The bull call spread will be worth $2.50 per share. Allowing for the small extra cost to establish this trade, the net gain is $3.30 per share [1.0 + 2.5 − .2 = 3.3], which is equivalent to a stock price of $19.80. Thus, you have reached slightly better than break-even with the stock recovering less than half of its loss.

Comment

In comparing Examples 1 and 2, note that the stock repair for 1 was done for a small credit, whereas 2 required a small debit. The explanation for this is the amount of time until the options expire (June versus May). To do the stock repair strategy for little or no cost, it typically requires options with at least two months until expiration. The more time allowed, the more likely a credit will be generated.

Stock Enhancement Strategy

Using the same concept as the stock repair strategy, you will see how to significantly enhance the return on a stock investment. The stock enhancement strategy uses options to expand the profit on your stock with no additional cost. A further enhanced return is achieved when a cheap surrogate is substituted for the stock.

Let's look at an example to illustrate the stock enhancement strategy:

- **Example 3.** In early March, you buy 100 shares of ZYX at $58 per share. Your plan is to hold this stock for the long-term with a target of $75.

  If your target is reached, that represents a nice profit of 29 percent. Let's see how we can do much better for no extra expense using stock enhancement:

  Trade: Buy 1 Jan 70 call for $3.70 per share and sell 2 Jan 75 calls for $2.50 per share. This produces a net credit of $1.30 per share [(2.5 × 2) − 3.7 = 1.3].

  Position: Along with an extra $1.3 per share in your account, you hold the combination of a covered call (long 100 shares of ZYX and short 1 Jan 75 call) and a bull call spread (long 1 Jan

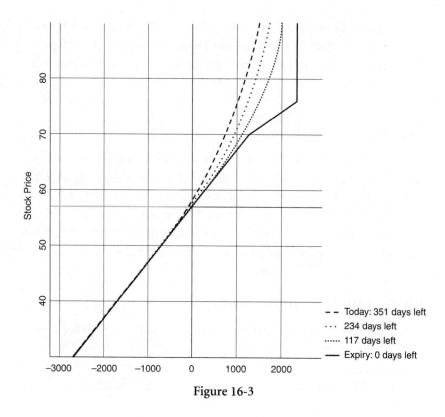

Figure 16-3

Legend:
- – – Today: 351 days left
- ··· 234 days left
- ······ 117 days left
- —— Expiry: 0 days left

70 call and short 1 Jan 75 call). See Figure 16-3 for a risk graph that depicts this position.

Payoff: If ZYX is above $75 in 10 months at the January options expiration, the stock will be called away at $75, for a $17 per share gain over its purchase price of $58. The bull call spread will be worth $5 per share. Including the initial credit, the total gain is $23.30 per share [17.0 + 5.0 + 1.3 = 23.3], which is equivalent to a stock price of $81.30. This represents a profit of 41 percent, even though the stock may have moved up by as little as 29 percent.

Modification: Instead of buying 100 shares of ZYX stock at $58 per share, buy 1 Jan 40 call for $19.70 per share. This option

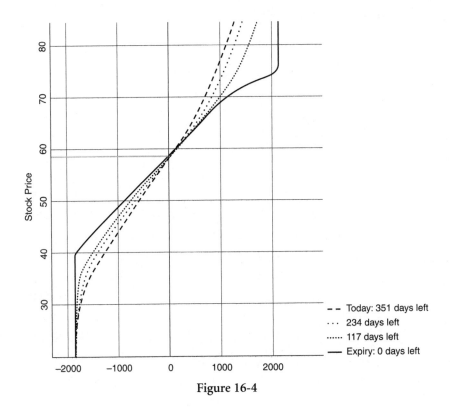

Figure 16-4

has a delta of .87, and hence its price will advance almost dollar for dollar with the stock price. In this case, the payoff at expiration if ZYX is above $75 will be $21.60 per share [(75.0 − 40.0) − 19.7 + 5.0 + 1.3 = 21.6]. This represents a profit of 110 percent based on the original cost of the Jan 40 call. See Figure. 16-4 for a risk graph that depicts this modification of Example 3.

17

MARRIED PUTS

Every time you buy a stock, you are exposing your investment capital to substantial risk. Fortunately, there is an inexpensive way to protect your investment while waiting for the stock to move up. This protection is established through an "arranged marriage" between your stock and an appropriate put option. In options terminology, this is known as the *married put strategy*.

As soon as you buy a stock, you are particularly anxious as you wait for it to begin moving upward. Obviously, you bought the stock because you believe its price is going up and you also believe that this upward move is going to happen soon. Even for disciplined investors, it is difficult to get rid of a nonperforming stock within the first few weeks after it is purchased. This means admitting you were either wrong about the stock or wrong about the timing, or both. So, all too frequently, we watch the price of our newly purchased stock drift downward as we try to assure ourselves that this is only a temporary setback and soon our rosy evaluation of this stock will be validated.

Many investors think that the solution to this situation is to use a stop loss order, which is set to trigger when the stock price moves down about 7 percent to 10 percent below the purchase price of the stock. There are two major problems with the stop loss approach: (1) If the stock gaps down, say 15 percent to 20 percent or more on some unexpected bad news, your stop loss will be executed at that much lower level. (2) Soon after you purchase the stock, it pulls back just enough to trigger the stop loss and then rebounds to a 15 percent gain. You will have been taken out of the trade and miss the opportunity to make a nice profit.

The married put strategy offers a way to avoid the problems posed by the stop loss order. It will allow you to hold your stock for several weeks (or longer) without concern for a pullback, while waiting for the anticipated move up in price. There are several variations of the married put strategy, but the one described here is the simplest and least expensive to employ.

The basic idea of the married put strategy is to buy an appropriate put option at the same time you purchase stock. Typically, a put is selected that will provide several weeks of protection against a downside move in the stock price, while you comfortably wait for the expected uptrend to begin. As the put nears its expiration date, some decision will have to be made about continuing to hold the stock. We examine several scenarios to see how an appropriate decision is reached.

Let's look at an example to see how the married put strategy works.

In late August, you decide to buy 100 shares of XYZ at $31 per share, because you are convinced that this stock will soon be headed toward $35 and perhaps much higher. For protection you also buy the Sept 30 put at $.80 per share.

> Trade: Buy 100 shares of XYZ at $31 a share and buy 1 contract of the Sept 30 put at $.80 per share.
>
> Cost = $(100 \times 31) + (100 \times .8) = \$3,180$.
>
> Max risk = $180.

See Figure 17-1 for a risk graph that depicts this trade.

Note that the maximum risk on this combination of the stock and the married put is only $180. Compare that with a maximum risk of $3,100 if the protective put is not in place.

How do we determine that the maximum risk is $180? If the stock is anywhere below $30 at any time before the September options expiration date, you can elect to exercise your option and sell your stock for $30 per share. That represents a loss of $1 per share on 100 shares for a total of $100. We must also include the expense of buying the put option at $.80 per share for a cost of $80 for the one contract. Thus, we obtain the maximum risk of $180 [100 + 80 = 180].

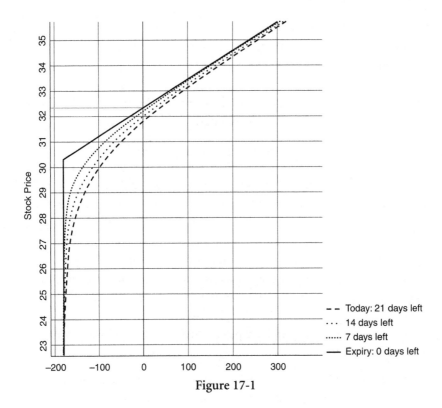

Figure 17-1

If some unexpected bad news on XYZ surfaces overnight and the stock opens at $25 on the following day, those who own 100 shares of stock without the married put will suffer an immediate loss of $600. Moreover, things might get even worse as the price of XYZ falls even further in the next few days. Do you sell or hang on with the hope of some recovery? This difficult question is of no concern if you own the Sept 30 put. You know that you cannot lose more than $180 no matter what happens to the stock. You can comfortably wait to see whether the bad news is reversed and the stock recovers to show a profit.

How is the appropriate put selected for protection of the stock? First, decide on the expiration month and then choose a strike price.

My recommendation for the choice of expiration month is the current month if there are at least three weeks remaining until expiration. If there are less than three weeks until expiration, use a put that expires the following month. In the latter case, you are going to have at least five weeks and possibly as many as seven weeks of protection. Avoid going out any further in time, because the options will be too expensive. The general idea here is to allow your stock between three and seven weeks to start showing the strength you are expecting.

As for the strike price, it is usually best to select the nearest strike price that is below the stock price, as illustrated in the preceding example. This way, you will only be paying for time value and that should not be too expensive since the option is never more than seven weeks from expiration. The exception to this choice is when the stock price is just below the next higher strike price. Then consider going to that higher strike option so as to provide sufficient protection. In the preceding example, suppose the purchase price for the XYZ stock had been $34. Then, the Sept 35 put at $1.90 per share might be a better choice to avoid $4 of risk in the stock price. The general idea here is to provide some protection of the purchase price of your stock without paying too much for the put.

What happens when the expiration date for the protective put arrives? This is when you will need to make a hard decision as to how you feel about this stock that interested you several weeks ago. You have had a chance to "test drive" this stock without concern. Now you must decide whether you really want to own it for the long term.

If the stock price has gone up, the decision will be easy. Before the put expires, initiate a stop loss order to protect some of your gain in the stock price. (Note that a stop loss order makes more sense now that there is some profit to act as a cushion.) This leaves you in a reasonable position to hold the stock for additional gains.

If the stock price has gone down, you have a choice of actions: (1) Get rid of the stock by exercising the put option, which enables you to sell the stock at the strike price. (2) If you want to continue holding this stock because it seems to have found its bottom, sell the put for a profit, thereby lowering the cost basis for the stock.

If the stock price has gone sideways, you might want to give serious thought to selling the stock and also selling the put if it has any residual value. To justify a decision to continue holding the stock, you will need to consider another married put. This means the stock will need to make an even larger gain to offset the expense of two protective puts—not usually an attractive scenario.

Comments

Here are some variations of the married put strategy:

- There are times to employ this strategy other than when you first buy a stock. Suppose you already own a stock that has provided a nice profit, but there is an upcoming special event (earnings report, FDA approval, court decision, and so on) that could send it into a steep decline. Use a married put to get past the special event. Then you will be much better placed to decide whether you should continue to hold the stock.

- For more-volatile stocks, the protective put that you would like to own may be rather expensive. You can reduce the cost by using a vertical Bear Put Spread instead of a simple protective put. To create the spread, buy the put you want for protection and then sell the one at the next-lower strike to offset the expense. There is risk with this approach, because the vertical bear spread can provide only limited protection.

- Another way to help finance the cost of the protective put is to sell a call at a strike price above the purchase price of the stock. This combination, known as a "collar," provides the desired protection, but it caps your upside profit. In Chapters 18, "Collars," and 19, "Advanced Collars," these collar trades are discussed in detail.

18

COLLARS

he *collar trade* has particular appeal to conservative investors. This is a trade for those who like to hold stocks for the long-term, while using options to provide insurance and still allow for a nice return. One reason the collar trade is so attractive is its high level of protection of principal.

During 2000 to 2002, there were many stocks that investors and analysts believed were good to hold for the long term. Unfortunately, a significant number of those "good stocks" lost 40 percent to 50 percent or even more of their value during that period of time. If those stocks whose price collapsed had been properly collared with options, the loss would have been held to less than 10 percent. And for those collared stocks that did manage to move up during the bear market, annualized returns of 15 percent to 25 percent were possible.

The collar trade is intended for use with stocks that are worthy of being held for at least 10 to 12 months. To do a collar trade, the stock needs to have LEAPS options associated with it. As discussed in Chapter 6, "LEAPS," these long-term options have expiration dates that may be as much as two years or more into the future.

Let's look at an example of a collar trade:

- **Example 1.** In November 2004, you identify XYZ as a stock worthy of being held for the next 14 months. XYZ is currently trading at $19 per share and it has LEAPS options.

  Trade: Buy 100 shares of XYZ for $1,900. Buy 1 Jan (06) 20 put for $2.90 per share and sell 1 Jan (06) 25 call for $1.00 per share. The net cost for the two options is

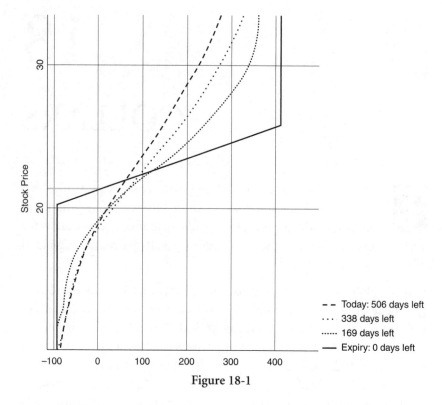

Figure 18-1

Legend:
- – – Today: 506 days left
- · · · 338 days left
- ······ 169 days left
- —— Expiry: 0 days left

$190 [(2.90 − 1.00) × 100 = 190]. The net cost for the whole trade is $2,090 [1,900 + 190 = 2,090].

See Figure 18-1 for a risk graph that depicts this trade.

Although it is possible to exit this trade at any time, it is designed to be held until the options expiration date in January 2006. Let's examine the best- and worst-case scenarios at expiration.

The worst-case scenario means that the stock price is below $20 on the options expiration date. In this situation, the Jan (06) 25 call expires worthless, while you exercise the Jan (06) 20 put to force someone to buy your stock at $20 per share. You receive $2,000 from the sale of your stock and your net loss on the trade is only $90 [2090 − 2000 = 90]. This small loss represents only 4.3 percent of your original investment.

The best-case scenario occurs when the stock price is over $25 on the option's expiration date. In this situation, the Jan (06) 20 put expires worthless and someone exercises the Jan (06) 25 call against you, so that your stock is sold for $25 per share. You receive $2,500 for your 100 shares of stock, and your net profit on the trade is $410 [2,500 − 2,090 = 410]. This represents a gain of 20 percent on your original investment. For the 14-month period that you are in this trade, that translates to a 17 percent gain on an annualized basis.

From Example 1, you can see why this combination of stock and options is called a collar trade. The two options form a "collar" around the long stock position. The long Jan (06) 20 put forms the protective part of the collar by insuring that the stock can be sold for no less than $20 per share anytime before the option expires. The Jan (06) 25 call, which was sold to reduce the cost of the put, forms the restrictive part of the collar that limits the upside selling price of the stock to $25 per share.

It is often possible to arrange the collar trade so that it is completely without risk. Usually, this will mean giving up some of the potential profit. Let's look at an example:

■ **Example 2.** As in Example 1, we will buy XYZ stock for $19 per share with the intention of holding it for the next 14 months. But now we will go for an even higher level of protection.

Trade: Buy 100 shares of XYZ for $1900. Buy 1 Jan (06) 22.5 put for $4.50 per share and sell 1 Jan (06) 25 call for $1 per share. The net cost of the two options is $350 [(4.50 − 1.00) × 100 = 350]. The net cost for the whole trade is $2,250 [1,900 + 350 = 2,250].

See Figure 18-2 for a risk graph that depicts this trade.

In this example, the worst-case scenario is the stock price below $22.50 on the option's expiration date. In this situation, the Jan (06) 25 call expires worthless, while you exercise the Jan (06) 22.5 put to force someone to buy your stock at $22.50 per share. You receive $2,250 from the sale of your stock, which is

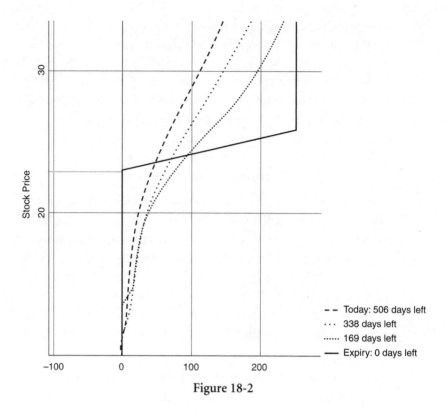

Figure 18-2

exactly the original cost of the trade, thereby allowing you to exit with no loss.

The best-case scenario is again when the price of XYZ is over $25 at expiration. The Jan (06) 22.5 put expires worthless and someone exercises the Jan (06) 25 call against you so that your stock is sold for $25 per share. You receive $2,500 for your 100 shares of stock and your net profit on the trade is $250 [2,500 − 2,250 = 250]. This represents a gain of 11 percent on your original investment. For the 14-month period that you are in this trade, that translates to a 9.5 percent gain on an annualized basis.

Although the maximum potential gain in Example 2 is significantly less than in Example 1, keep in mind that the collar trade in Example 2 carries no risk of principal. This may be particularly important for someone whose portfolio includes a large holding in XYZ stock.

If you are willing to accept a little more risk, the collar can be loosened to allow for a larger profit potential, as Example 3 shows.

■ **Example 3.** As in the previous two examples, we buy XYZ stock for $19 per share with the intention of holding it for the next 14 months. But now we go for a higher maximum return while accepting a little more risk.

Trade: Buy 100 shares of XYZ for $1,900. Buy 2 Jan (06) 20 put for $2.90 per share and sell 1 Jan (06) 30 call for $.60 per share. The net cost for the 2 options is $230 [(2.90 − .60) × 100 = 230]. The net cost for the whole trade is $2,130 [1,900 + 230 = 2,130].

See Figure 18-3 for a risk graph that depicts this trade.

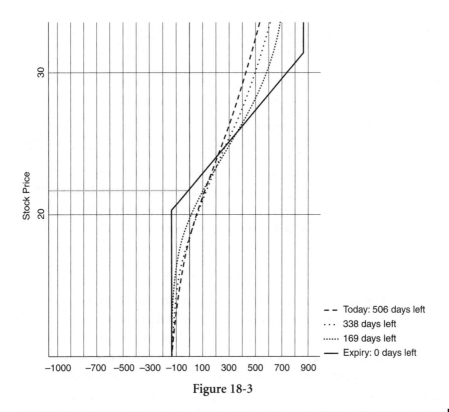

Figure 18-3

As in Example 1, the worst-case scenario is the stock price below $20 on the option's expiration date. In this situation, the Jan (06) 30 call expires worthless, while you exercise the Jan (06) 20 put to force someone to buy your stock at $20 per share. You receive $2,000 from the sale of your stock, and your net loss on the trade is $130 [2,130 – 2,000 = 130]. This loss represents 6.1 percent of your original investment.

The best-case scenario occurs again when the stock price is over $30 on the option's expiration date. In this situation, the Jan (06) 20 put expires worthless, and someone exercises the Jan (06) 30 call against you, so that your stock is sold for $30 per share. You receive $3,000 for your 100 shares of stock and your net profit on the trade is $870 [3,000 – 2,130 = 870]. This represents a gain of 41 percent on your original investment. For the 14-month period that you are in this trade, that translates to a 35 percent gain on an annualized basis.

In this example, the maximum gain is significantly better than that of Example 1, but the maximum loss has been increased.

Let's reconsider the Example 1 trade and see the difference if we extend that trade for an additional 12 months.

- **Example 4.** As in Example 1, we buy XYZ stock for $19 per share. But now the intention is to hold it for the next 26 months.

  Trade: Buy 100 shares of XYZ stock for $1,900. Buy 1 Jan (07) 20 put for $3.40 per share and sell 1 Jan (07) 25 call for $2.30 per share. The net cost for the 2 options is $110 [(3.40 – 2.30) × 100 = 110]. The net cost for the whole trade is $2010 [1,900 + 110 = 2,010].

  See Figure 18-4 for a risk graph that depicts this trade.

  The worst-case scenario means that the stock price is below $20 on the option's expiration date. In this situation, the Jan (07) 25 call expires worthless, while you exercise the Jan (07) 20 put to force someone to buy your stock at $20 per share. You receive $2,000 from the sale of your stock and your

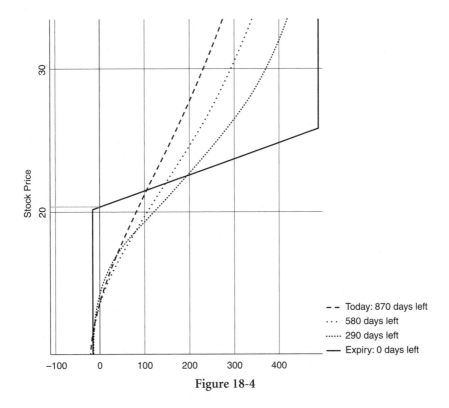

Figure 18-4

net loss on the trade is only $10 [2,010 − 2,000 = 10]. This small loss represents only 0.5 percent of your original investment. This is essentially a riskless trade.

The best-case scenario occurs when the stock price is over $25 on the option's expiration date. In this situation, the Jan (07) 20 put expires worthless and someone exercises the Jan (07) 25 call against you, so that your stock is sold for $25 per share. You receive $2,500 for your 100 shares of stock, and your net profit on the trade is $490 [2,500 − 2,010 = 490]. This represents a gain of 24 percent on your original investment. For the 26-month period that you are in this trade, that translates to an 11 percent return on an annualized basis.

It is worthwhile to compare Examples 1 and 4. We see that by going to a longer-term scenario, the trade becomes essentially riskless. The maximum potential profit has increased slightly, although the return on an annualized basis is less. The trade in Example 4 would appeal to a conservative investor who is willing to accept a modest return when his investment capital is almost fully protected from loss.

Comments

Collar trades are designed to be long-term trades. Trying to set up a collar trade for a period of less than 10 to 12 months will not provide the level of protection seen in the examples presented here.

Because the collar trades use LEAPS options, they generally can be structured for 22 to 24 months duration if so desired. With the longer duration, the maximum potential gain and maximum loss are typically better than the 10-to-12-month versions of the collar trade, as seen by comparing Examples 1 and 4. A major drawback to the 22-to-24-months collar trade is the cap placed on the upward price movement of the stock. If your stock is well above the strike price of the short call after 12 months, you will not be pleased that your profit is already capped while it will take another 10 to 12 months before the maximum return is achieved.

It is possible to exit a collar trade early; however, to achieve the maximum return generally requires staying in the trade until expiration. In Example 1, if XYZ reaches $25 with six months remaining until expiration, the profit would be only about half of the $410 maximum. When the stock price falls, it is often possible to exit the collar trade early for a slightly smaller loss than the maximum.

The collar trade is enhanced if the stock pays a dividend. In Example 1, suppose that XYZ pays an annual dividend of $.65 per share. That represents an annualized yield of 3.4 percent, which is equivalent to 4.0 percent for the 14-month duration of the collar. This means that the maximum return on the trade in Example 1 is increased to 24 percent, whereas the maximum loss has been reduced to a miniscule 0.3 percent.

Collar trades on highly volatile stocks are generally not as appealing as they are for more conservative stocks. The higher volatility will usually result in a much greater net cost for the options that provide the collar. This will increase the maximum possible loss on the trade.

19*

ADVANCED COLLARS

In this chapter, we consider some variations of the standard collar trades that were presented in Chapter 18, "Collars." These variations do introduce some additional risk with the goal of enhancing the return.

Let's consider a variation of Example 1 in Chapter 18 that introduces a deep-in-the-money call with a high delta as a substitute for stock.

- **Example 1A.** In November 2004, you are interested in holding XYZ stock for the next 14 months. Instead of buying the stock at $19 per share, the Jan (06) 10 call is used as a substitute for the stock. The Jan (06) call is priced at $9.60 per share. This option is a good surrogate for XYZ stock because it has a delta of .95 and its time value is only $.60 per share [(10.00 + 9.60) − 19.00 = .60].

  Trade: Buy 1 Jan (06) 10 call for $9.60 per share as a substitute for 100 shares of XYZ stock. As before, buy 1 Jan (06) 20 put for $2.90 per share and sell 1 Jan (06) 25 call for $1.00 per share. The net cost of the three options is $1,150 [(9.60 + 2.90 − 1.00) × 100 = 1,150].

  See Figure 19-1 for a risk graph that depicts this trade.

  For this collar trade, the worst-case scenario is not as simple to describe, because we have substituted an option for stock. The maximum loss is incurred at the option's expiration date if the stock price is below $20 but above $10, as seen in Figure 19-1. In this situation, the Jan (06) 25 call expires worthless, while the net value of the Jan (06) 10 call and the Jan (06) 20 put will be

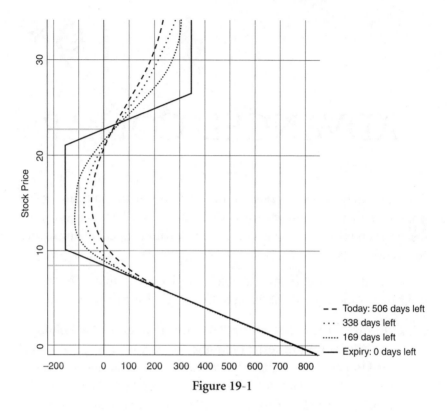

Figure 19-1

exactly $10 per share. This allows you to cash out those two
options for $1,000, resulting in a loss of $150 [1,150 − 1,000 =
150]. This represents a loss of 13 percent of the original
investment.

If the stock price is above $25 at the option's expiration date,
the Jan (06) 20 put expires worthless. The long Jan (06) 10 call
and the short Jan (06) 25 call constitute a Bull Call Spread with
a value of $1,500 [(25 − 10) × 100 = 1,500]. The net profit is
then $350 [1,500 − 1,150 = 350]. This represents a gain of
30 percent on your original investment. For the 14-month
period that you are in this trade, that translates to a 26 percent
return on an annualized basis.

It is an interesting anomaly of this trade that the largest potential profit is realized if the stock price is significantly below $10

at the option's expiration date, as seen in Figure 19-1. Suppose the XYZ stock price had dropped to $3. Then the Jan (06) 10 call would expire worthless, while the Jan (06) 20 put would be worth $17 per share. Selling that put for $1,700 [(20 − 3) × 100 = 1,700] results in a profit of $550 [1,700 − 1,150 = 550]. This represents a profit of 48 percent. If the price of XYZ fell all the way to 0, the profit would expand to 74 percent.

Let's consider another variation of Example 1 in Chapter 18 that introduces some short-term risk in an effort to reduce the cost of the collar.

■ **Example 1B.** In November 2004, you buy XYZ stock for $19 per share with the intention of holding it for the next 14 months. The standard collar trade is amended by also selling a near-term put to reduce the cost basis of the long-term put.

Trade: Buy 100 shares of XYZ stock for $1,900. Buy 1 Jan (06) 20 put for $2.90 per share and sell 1 Jan (06) 25 call for $1 per share. Additionally, sell 1 Dec (04) 17.5 put for $.70 per share. The net cost of the three options is $120 [(2.90 − 1.00 − .70) × 100 = 120]. The net cost for the whole trade is $2,020 [1,900 + 120 = 2,020].

See Figure 19-2 for a risk graph that depicts this trade.

The idea here is to collect some short-term premium by selling the Dec (04) 17.5 put. The Jan (06) put serves as a hedge for the short Dec (04) 17.5 put in case the stock price falls. Of course, this means that the Jan (06) put is not fully available to protect the 100 shares of XYZ stock until the December put expires in about 6 weeks. The increased downside risk is seen in Figure 19-2. Under these circumstances, it is wise to initiate a stop loss order on the stock until the December put expires.

Assuming that the Dec (04) 17.5 put expires worthless, the original trade then reverts to a standard collar trade with a reduced cost basis of $2,020. See Figure 19-3 for a risk graph that depicts that trade.

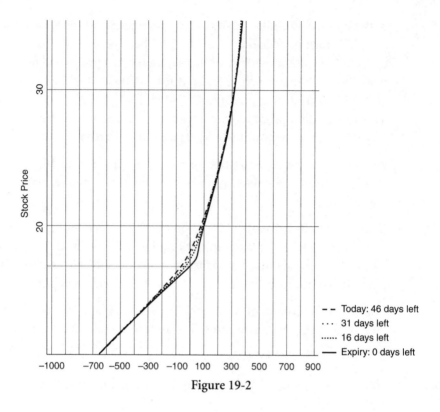

Figure 19-2

For this updated collar trade, the worst-case scenario at the January 2006 option's expiration is a loss of only $20 [2,020 – 2,000 = 20], as seen in Figure 19-3. This represents a maximum loss of only 1.0 percent based on the reduced cost of the trade.

The maximum potential profit from the collar trade also benefits from the premium collected from the Dec (04) 17.5 put. If XYZ is above $25 at the January 2006 option's expiration, the net profit is $480 [2,500 – 2,020 = 480]. This represents a gain of 24 percent on the original investment.

Clearly, the drawback to this variation is the six weeks of exposure while waiting for the short Dec (04) 17.5 put to expire. If the price of XYZ is only slightly below $17.50 at the December 2004 option's expiration, it may be possible to roll the Dec (04) 17.5 put into the Jan (05) 15 put for a small loss.

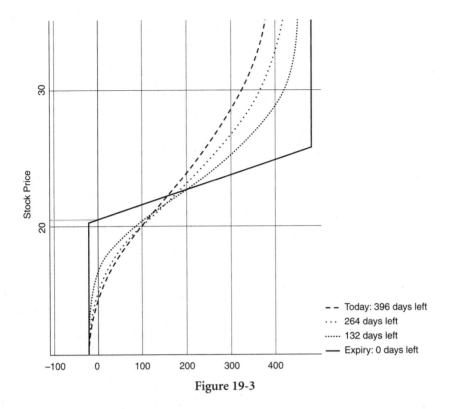

Figure 19-3

Let's consider another modification of the collar trade that allows for unlimited profit with only a small increase in the risk. This strategy requires the purchase of more than 100 shares of stock. The idea is to sell fewer calls than corresponds to the total shares of stock owned. This will free up some shares of stock for unlimited gain.

- **Example 1C.** In November 2004, you buy 400 shares of XYZ stock for $19 per share with the intention of holding it for the next 14 months. As in the standard collar trade, puts are purchased to protect all 400 shares of the stock. But calls are sold against only 300 shares of the stock. This combination allows for 100 shares of stock to remain uncapped by the presence of a short call.

Trade: Buy 400 shares of XYZ stock at $19 per share for a total of $7,600. Buy 4 Jan (06) 20 puts for $2.90 per share and sell 3

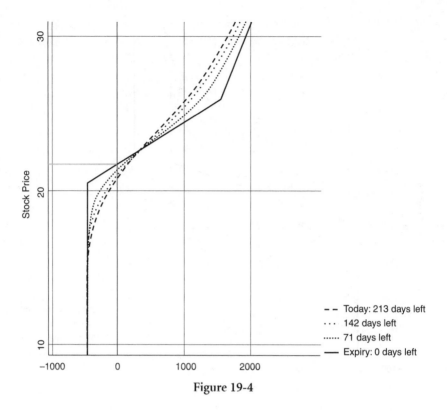

Figure 19-4

Jan (06) 25 calls for $1 per share. The net cost of this trade is $8,460 [7,600 + (2.90 × 400) − (1.00 × 300) = 8,460.

See Figure 19-4 for a risk graph that depicts this trade.

The worst-case scenario means that the stock price is below $20 on the option's expiration date. In this situation, the 3 Jan (06) 25 calls expire worthless, while you exercise the 4 Jan (06) 20 puts to force someone to buy your 400 shares of stock at $20 per share. You receive $8,000 from the sale of your stock and your net loss on the trade is $460 [8,460 − 8,000 = 460]. This represents a loss of 5.4 percent of your original investment.

The best-case scenario for this trade is an unlimited return on the 100 shares of stock that are uncapped by the short calls. For example, if the stock price is at $32 on the option's expiration date, the 4 Jan (06) 20 puts expire worthless and someone exercises the 3 Jan (06) 25 call against you, so that 300 shares of your stock are sold for $25 per share. The remaining 100 shares of stock can be sold for $3,200. The net profit on the trade is $2,240 [(25 × 300) + (32 × 100) − 8,460 = 2,240]. This represents a gain of 26 percent on your original investment. For the 14-month period that you are in this trade, that translates to a 23 percent gain on an annualized basis.

It should be noted that the unencumbered 100 shares of stock can be sold at anytime before the expiration date, if the stock price has risen sufficiently to warrant that action. If those 100 shares are sold, one of the protective puts is no longer needed and can be sold for whatever residual value remains.

Comments

The key to understanding the collar trade is the realization that long-term calls have more time value than comparable long-term puts. And the more distant the expiration date, the larger is this difference. An explanation of this disparity in the pricing of call and put options is given in Chapter 30, "The Put-Call Parity Relationship." Thus, selling an out-of-the-money long-term call provides extra cash to offset the purchase price of an at-the-money put. This explains why short or intermediate-term collar trades are generally unattractive.

The maximum potential loss on a collar trade is reduced by moving the strike prices of the call and put options closer together. Unfortunately, this adjustment also reduces the maximum potential profit. The strike price of the short call must always exceed that of the long put for a profit to be possible.

20

NAKED OPTION
WRITING

A s you learn about options, there will come a time when you consider *naked option writing*. This type of trading can be rewarding, but before trying it, you need to be fully aware of the risks involved in selling naked calls and naked puts.

The word *naked* is defined in the Funk & Wagnalls Dictionary as "having no covering . . ."; this is a particularly relevant description of naked option writing. When you sell either a call or a put without any compensating position to "cover" the short option, you are said to be "naked." By having a short naked call or naked put position in your brokerage account, you are exposed to substantial risk. So, it is important to be prepared to manage this type of trade if the underlying stock begins to move against you.

In the late 1990s, there were some so-called investment gurus who advised that the quick way to great wealth was to sell out-of-the-money naked options. They argued that the vast majority of these out-of-the-money options expire worthless every month and therefore the risk is minimal. At that time, the emphasis was on selling puts because the prices of tech stocks were soaring, thereby causing more and more puts to expire worthless as the Nasdaq moved steadily upward. When the tech bubble burst in 2000, there were disastrous consequences for those gurus and their followers, whose naked put positions incurred massive losses.

Because most brokerage firms forbid naked option writing in a retirement account, this issue may seem irrelevant to people who only trade in that type of account. It is interesting, however, that almost all brokers do permit covered call strategies in retirement accounts, because a covered call carries exactly the same risk as a naked put. This was demonstrated in Chapter 14, "Covered Calls."

The goal of this chapter is to make you aware of the potential risks as well as the potential rewards of selling naked calls and puts. Let's begin with the risks.

The Risk of Naked Option Writing

You will often hear that selling a naked option exposes you to "unlimited risk." Although this is not literally true, the risk can be large enough to cause considerable loss in you brokerage account. To realistically illustrate the magnitude of the risk, we will consider some actual market situations where substantial losses were generated for those traders who sold naked options.

- **Example 1.** Naked put

  In early June 2004, OVTI stock was moving up nicely as the earnings announcement scheduled for June 9 was approaching. Many analysts expected the announcement to reveal that the profits of this high profile company were continuing to grow as had been reported in the past. With the stock trading a little over $25 on June 8, it was certainly tempting to sell a few June 25 puts naked for $1 per share.

  Suppose that on June 8 you sold 5 Jun 25 puts naked to bring $500 cash into your account. This looked like easy money because the stock price seemed likely to continue upward, or at least stay level, following the expected rosy earnings report. Also, these options would expire in only two and a half weeks on June 18, which meant that you did not have long to wait for the capture of the $500 credit to be completed. See Figure 20-1 for a risk graph that depicts this trade on June 8.

  After the market closed on June 8, OVTI issued a statement that its earnings announcement would be delayed until June 23

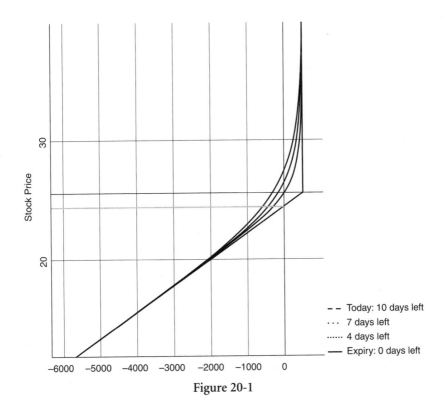

Figure 20-1

due to an internal investigation regarding the need to restate its earnings for the past year. On June 9, the stock opened at $19 and continued trading down until it closed at $15.50 as the options expired on June 18. At this point, you would have to decide between two unpleasant choices: (1) Buy back the 5 short puts for $9.50 per share, or (2) accept the assignment to buy 500 shares of the stock at $25 per share. In either case, the value of your brokerage account was diminished by $4,250. The reason for this massive loss was that the short Jun 25 puts were naked. They were not covered by any other position to limit the risk.

See Figure 20-2 for a risk graph that depicts this situation on June 18.

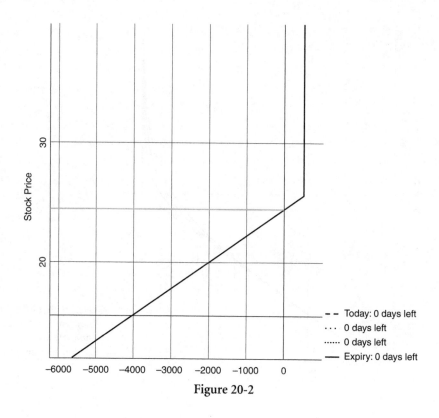

Figure 20-2

- **Example 2.** Naked call

  In early June 2004, CYBX stock was trading at $18. The rumor surrounding this company was that an FDA panel might disapprove its implant device to treat severely depressed patients. The Jun 20 calls were trading at $3.50 per share. It seemed that selling a few of these calls naked might be profitable, because some analysts projected that the stock price would only move up a few dollars even if the implant device was approved.

  Suppose that on Jun 10 you sold three Jun 20 calls naked to bring $1,050 cash into your account.

  See Figure 20-3 for a risk graph that depicts this trade on June 10.

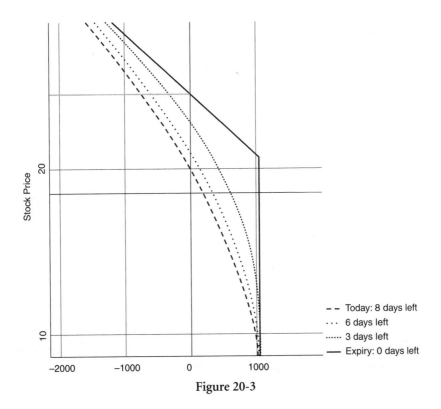

Figure 20-3

After the close of trading on June 15, just three days before the options were to expire, CYBX announced that the implant device had been approved by the FDA panel. The next day, CYBX opened at $31, and by the expiration date of June 18, the stock was at $37. At this point, you would have to decide between two unpleasant choices: (1) Buy back the 3 short calls for $19 per share, or (2) wait for the assignment on the following Monday and be forced to buy 300 shares of CYBX stock at $37 (possibly even higher) and deliver it at $20. In either case, you would see an immediate reduction in the value of your brokerage account by an amount of $4,650.

Again, the reason for this massive loss was that the short Jun 20 calls were naked. They were not covered by any other position to limit the risk.

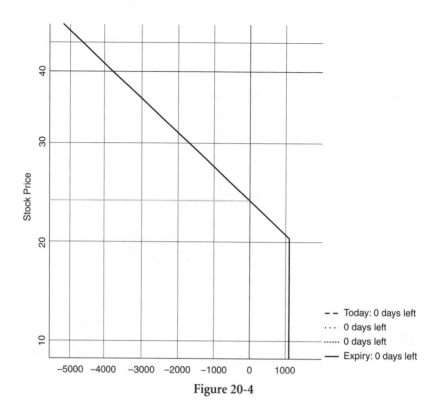

Figure 20-4

See Figure 20-4 for a risk graph that depicts this situation on June 18.

Now that you have been sufficiently warned about the danger of naked option writing, let's look at one situation in which it might be an acceptable strategy.

Acquiring Stock with Naked Puts

Let's see how naked puts can be used as a strategy to acquire a good stock at a desirable price. An example will be used to illustrate this strategy:

- **Example 3.** Suppose that you have carefully researched XYZ stock. You believe that buying 200 shares of this stock would be a sound investment for the future. XYZ is currently selling for $31 per share, and although you are prepared to buy the stock at that price, it would be nice to get it for a little less.

You note that the front month $30 puts are being sold at $1.25 per share. If you sell two of these puts naked, this brings $250 into your brokerage account. By being naked in those 2 puts, you must be prepared to buy 200 shares of the stock at $30 if necessary. This must be regarded as acceptable, because you were already prepared to purchase the stock for $31.

When the front-month options expire, there are two possible outcomes to consider:

1. If XYZ is above $30, the short puts expire worthless and you keep the $250. If it still seems like a good investment to acquire this stock, you can repeat the process for the following month. Otherwise, you move on to another stock of interest.

2. If XYZ is below $30, the short puts will be exercised and you will be required to buy the 200 shares for $30 per share. Your actual cost basis for the stock is only $28.75 per share because of the $1.25 per share that you received from the sale of the puts.

If XYZ had experienced a pullback to $29, you would still be buying the stock for an equivalent price of $28.75 per share. Note how this is much better than having bought the stock at $31 per share when you initially decided to acquire this stock.

It is wise to have some sort of stop loss strategy in mind when selling naked options. Think of this as the same as initiating stop loss when you buy the stock. In the preceding example, if XYZ was at $31 when you sold the naked put, your mental stop loss might be at $28, which represents a 10 percent pullback in the stock price. So, if XYZ falls to $28, buy back the naked put for, say, $2.60 per share. This represents a loss of $1.35 per share [2.60 − 1.25 = 1.35]. Notice that this is a significant improvement over a loss of $3 per share that would have been realized if the stock had been purchased at $31.

21

STOCK SUBSTITUTES

As discussed in Chapter 20, "Naked Option Writing," there is substantial risk in trades that involve uncovered short options. Nevertheless, in some circumstances, it is worthwhile to consider naked positions. In this chapter, we examine some situations in which you can use naked puts and calls as cheap substitutes for stock.

Synthetic Long Stock

An at-the-money long call has a delta = 0.5, whereas an at-the-money short (naked) put has a delta = –(–0.5) = 0.5. When held as a unit, the combination of a long call and a short put, with the same at-the-money strike price, has a delta of 1.0 [0.5 – (–0.50) = 1.0]. Because long stock has a delta of 1.0, this combination of options is known as *synthetic stock*. What makes this combination particularly appealing is that its net cost is almost zero. The premium received from selling the naked put will come very close to paying for the long call.

Although the net cost of the synthetic stock position is nearly zero, it does come with some strings attached. Your broker will require some margin to maintain this position, because of the naked put, but that is typically far less than the cost of owning the real stock. The margin required by brokerage firms varies, but a rule of thumb is 25 percent of the underlying stock (or index) price plus the price of the option if the option is in-the-money. If the option is out-of-the-money, that margin figure is reduced by the amount that the option is out-of-the-money.

Let's look at an example to illustrate synthetic long stock:

- **Example 1.** In early June, XYZ stock is trading at $76. To participate in the movement of this stock over the next three months, October options are selected. The nearest strike price is $75. Here is the trade that establishes the synthetic stock position:

Trade: Buy 1 Oct 75 call for $4.50 per share and sell 1 Oct 75 put for $2.70, for a net cost of $1.80 per share.

Cost = $180.

Max risk = Essentially the same as the max loss from stock ownership.

This synthetic stock position was created by using options with a $75 strike price. This means that all gains and losses in the synthetic stock are referenced to $75. With the current price of XYZ at $76, this suggests that the cost of this synthetic stock should ideally be $1 per share. The actual cost of $1.80 per share contains an extra $.80, which represents the time value cost of holding this position.

See Figure 21-1 for a risk graph that depicts this trade.

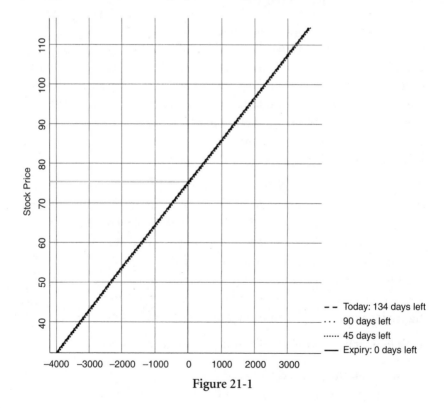

Figure 21-1

To calculate the margin requirement on the preceding trade, notice that the naked put is out-of-the-money by $1. Therefore, the margin required is 25 percent of the XYZ stock price plus the price of the Oct 75 put less the amount the option is out-of-the-money. In this case, the margin on one contract would be $2,070 {[(.25 × 76.00) + 2.70 − 1.00] × 100 = 2,070}. This margin requirement of $2,070 for the synthetic stock is considerably less than the $7,600 cost of owning 100 shares of the stock. Note that the margin requirement is not fixed, but changes daily as the stock and option prices change.

From Figure 21-1, you can see that the profit and loss on this trade is exactly the same as stock that was purchased for $76.80.

Comments

There are some drawbacks to synthetic stock. If the real stock pays dividends, this surrogate does not get a penny. And if the stock price were to fall so far that the naked put becomes deep-in-the-money, there is the possibility of an early assignment. When there is an assignment of real stock, the synthetic position has been dismantled. Another minor drawback is that when the options expire, a new synthetic position needs to be established if you want to continue participating in the stock price movement.

A synthetic position that is equivalent to a short stock position is created by buying a put and selling a call with the same strike price. Unlike shorting a stock, very little if any cash will be credited to your brokerage account. The margin required to hold the position will be based on the naked short call.

Deep-in-the-Money Put

A short *deep-in-the-money naked put* will have a delta very close to one. This makes this position a viable substitute for stock. As the stock moves up in price, this position will capture the move almost dollar for dollar, until the stock price nears the strike price of the short put. An attractive feature of this stock surrogate is the large amount of cash brought into your brokerage account from the sale of the very expensive put. This cash earns interest as it sits in your account.

This naked put position will require margin in your brokerage account, but still should not tie up nearly as much capital as owning the real stock. The main disadvantage to this stock substitute is the possibility of an early assignment. Even though a naked put has an expiration date in the distant future, it may have almost no time value included in its price when it becomes very deep-in-the-money. This makes it vulnerable to early assignment. If assigned, you can always reestablish the position, but that can become tiresome and expensive because the commission costs add up after several assignments. The best way to avoid this problem is to pick a strike price not too deep-in-the-money, so that the put price still includes some time value. Also, check the open interest of the option. With a large open interest, the possibility of an early assignment is diminished.

Let's look at an example:

- **Example 2.** In early June, XYZ stock is trading at $76. To participate in the (upward) movement of this stock over the next three months, an October put is selected.

  Trade: Sell 1 Oct 90 put for $14.80 per share.

  Credit = $1,480.

  Max risk = Essentially the same as the max loss from stock ownership.

Note that the option selected has a time value of $.80 per share [(76.00 + 14.80) − 90.00 = 0.80]. This time value together with an ample open interest (say, at least 300 contracts) would mean that the chance for an early assignment is unlikely.

See Figure 21-2 for a risk graph that depicts this trade.

To calculate the margin requirement on this trade, notice that the naked put is in-the-money. Therefore, the margin required is 25 percent of the XYZ stock price plus the price of the Oct 90 put. In this case, the margin on one contract would be $3,380 {[(.25 × 76.00) + 14.80] × 100 = 3,380}. This margin requirement of $3,380 is not as expensive as it first

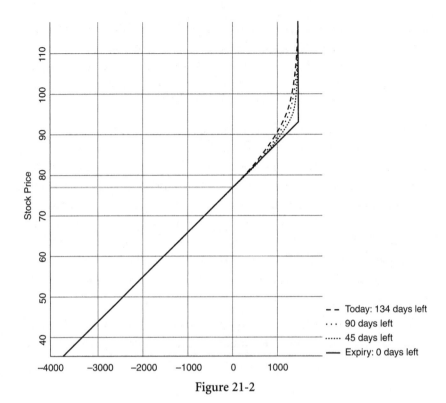

Figure 21-2

seems, because the $1,480 cash brought into your account from the sale of the put is used to meet the requirement. Thus, the effective margin requirement is only $1,900, which is considerably less than the $7,600 cost of owning 100 shares of the stock. Again, the margin requirement is not fixed, but changes as the stock and option prices change.

A disadvantage of this naked put strategy is that its maximum profit is limited to the amount of money received from the sale of the put. If the stock price closes above the strike price of the put at expiration, there will not be any additional profit related to the amount that the stock price exceeds the strike price (as shown in Figure 21-2).

Deep-in-the-Money Call

A short *deep-in-the-money naked call* will have a delta very close to minus one. This makes this position a viable substitute for short stock.

As the stock moves down in price, this position will capture the move almost dollar-for-dollar, until the stock price nears the strike price of the short call. As with shorting the actual stock, this short stock surrogate brings cash into your brokerage account from the sale of the expensive call. This cash earns interest as it sits in your account.

This naked call position will require margin in your brokerage account, but still should not tie up nearly as much capital as shorting the real stock. The possibility of an early assignment is somewhat less than for the naked put position previously described, because calls always tend to have more time value than puts. Also, with a large open interest, the possibility of an early assignment is diminished. One situation that does make the possibility of early assignment more likely is when a stock pays a dividend. The owners of deep-in-the-money calls will often exercise them before expiration when that action leads to the receipt of a dividend.

This strategy for a synthetic short stock using naked calls is less often used because it does not offer much advantage over shorting the real stock.

Let's look at an example:

- **Example 3**. In early May, XYZ stock is trading at $76. To participate in the downward movement of this stock over the next three months, an October call is selected.

  Trade: Sell 1 Oct 60 call for $16.90 per share.

  Credit = $1,690.

  Max risk = Essentially the same as the max loss from shorting the stock.

Note that the option selected has a time value of $.90 per share [60.00 − (76.00 − 16.90) = 0.90]. This time value together with an ample open interest (say, at least 300 contracts) means that the chance for an early assignment is unlikely.

See Figure 21-3 for a risk graph that depicts this trade.

To calculate the margin requirement on this trade, notice that the naked call is in-the-money. Therefore, the margin required is 25 percent of

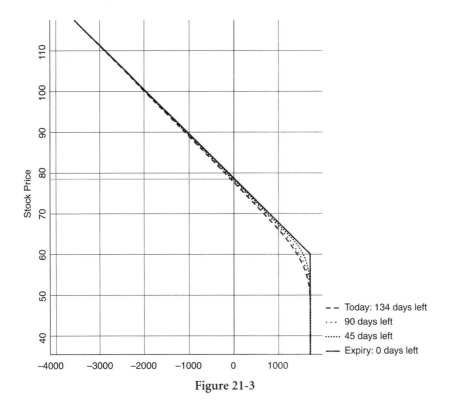

Figure 21-3

the XYZ stock price plus the price of the Oct 60 call. In this case, the margin on one contract would be $3,590 $\{[(.25 \times 76.00) + 16.90] \times 100 = 3,590\}$. As in the previous example, this margin requirement of $3,590 is effectively reduced to $1,900 because of the $1,690 cash brought into your account from the sale of the call. Again, the margin requirement is not fixed, but changes as the stock and option prices change.

A disadvantage of this naked call strategy is that its maximum profit is limited to the amount of money received from the sale of the call. If the stock price manages to be below the strike price of the short call at expiration, there will not be any additional profit based on the amount that the strike price exceeds the stock price, as shown in Figure 21-3.

22

BACKSPREADS

The *backspread trade* is used to take advantage of large moves (up or down) in the price of a stock or index. A backspread trade consists of more long options than short options with the strike prices selected so that the cost of the spread is small and even sometimes can be initiated for a credit.

The main drawback to a backspread trade is that it returns a significant profit only for large moves in the underlying stock or index. In fact, the spread incurs its maximum loss when the stock or index has achieved only a modest move in price at the option's expiration date.

Let's begin by looking at a typical example of a bullish backspread trade:

- **Example 1.** In February, XYZ stock is at $19, and you feel that this stock has the possibility of being at $35 or higher within the next year. To take advantage of this potentially large move at little cost, you consider a backspread trade that uses LEAPS calls that will expire in about 11 months.

  Trade: Buy 2 Jan 22.5 calls at $1.70 per share, and sell 1 Jan 20 call at $2.80 per share.

  Cost = $60 [2(1.70 × 100) − (2.80 × 100) = 60].

  Max risk = $310.

See Figure 22-1 for a risk graph that depicts this trade.

To better understand this backspread trade, it is useful to think of it as a combination of (1) one long Jan 22.5 call purchased for $1.70 per share and (2) a bear call spread composed of one long Jan 22.5 call and

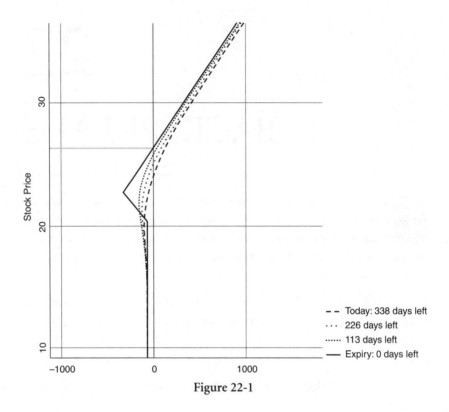

Figure 22-1

Today: 338 days left
··· 226 days left
······ 113 days left
—— Expiry: 0 days left

one short Jan call, which generates a credit of $1.10 per share [2.80 − 1.70 = 1.10]. The idea here is that the credit spread is being used to finance the cost of the long call.

At expiration, if XYZ is anywhere above $22.5, the cost of closing the credit spread will be $250 [(22.5 − 20.0) × 100 = 250]. The one unencumbered Jan 22.5 call can realize unlimited profit. The break-even point for the trade at expiration is XYZ at $25.60. At that point, the long call has a profit of $310 [(25.60 − 22.50) × 100 = 310]. This exactly offsets the $250 cost of closing the credit spread along with the original $60 cost to initiate the trade.

Suppose that XYZ has risen to $35 as the January option's expiration date arrives. The net profit on the trade is the profit that the unencumbered call makes beyond its break-even price of $25.60. In this case, the profit is $940 [(35.00 − 25.60) × 100 = 940]. The return on this trade relative to maximum risk is 269 percent.

The maximum risk on the above trade is $310. This corresponds to XYZ closing at exactly $22.50 at expiration, as seen in Figure 22-1. Then the two long calls expire worthless, and the short call must be bought back for $250 [(22.5 − 20.0) × 100 = 2.5]. This loss of $250 in addition to the original cost of $60 to initiate the trade gives a total loss of $310. If XYZ closes above $22.50, the long calls have some value to offset the cost of buying back the short call. If XYZ closes below $22.50, it costs less to buy back the short call. If XYZ closes below $20, the short call expires worthless and the loss is limited to the $60 cost to initiate the trade.

Next, let's look at an example of a bearish backspread trade where we start out with a credit:

- **Example 2.** In October, ZYX is flying high with a price of $76. You feel that this stock is sure to fall back to the level of $45 over the next several months. Consider playing this scenario with a backspread trade using March puts, which expire in six months.

  Trade: Buy 2 Mar 65 puts at $4.20 per share and sell 1 Mar 75 put at $9.60 per share.

  Initial credit = $120 [(9.6 × 100) − 2(4.2 × 100) = 120].

  Max risk = $880.

See Figure 22-2 for a risk graph that depicts this trade.

This trade can be thought of as a combination of (1) one long Mar 65 put purchased for $4.20 per share and (2) a bull put spread composed of one long Mar 65 put and one short Mar 75 put, which generates a credit of $5.40 per share [9.6 − 4.2 = 5.4]. The credit more than pays for the long put, leaving us a net credit of $120 on the combination.

At expiration, if ZYX is anywhere below $65, the cost of closing the credit spread will be $1,000 [(75.0 − 65.0) × 100 = 1,000]. The one unencumbered Mar 65 put can realize unlimited profit. The break-even point for this trade at expiration is ZYX at $56.20. At that point, the long put has a profit of $880 [(65.0 − 56.2) × 100 = 880]. This profit

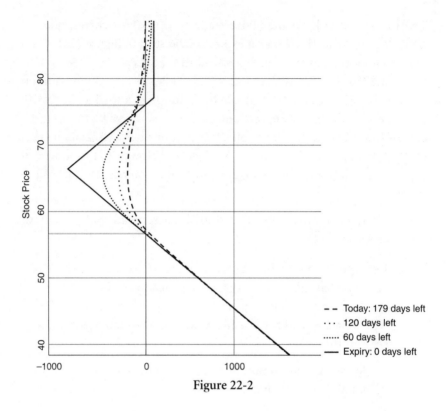

Figure 22-2

together with the initial credit of $120 exactly offsets the $1,000 cost of closing the credit spread.

Suppose that ZYX has fallen to $45 as the March 2005 option's expiration date arrives. The net profit on the put backspread trade is the profit that the unencumbered put makes beyond its break-even price of $56.20. In this case, the profit is $1,120 [(56.20 − 45.00) × 100 = 1,120]. The return on this trade relative to maximum risk is 127 percent.

The maximum risk on the above trade is $880. This corresponds to ZYX closing at exactly $65 at expiration. Then, the two long puts expire worthless, and the short put must be bought back for 1,000 [(75.0 − 65.0) × 100 = 1,000]. This loss of $1,000 is offset by the original credit of $120 to cause a net loss of $880. If ZYX closes below $65, the long puts have some value to offset the cost of buying back the short put. If ZYX closes above $65, it costs less to buy back the short put.

If ZYX closes above $75, the short put expires worthless, and we have a net profit on the trade from the original credit received of $120. So, if you are completely wrong about this high-flying stock and it fails to fall over the next six months, this spread yields a small profit.

The basic concept of the backspread trade is to finance a long option by combining it with a credit spread. The standard version of the trade uses a ratio of two long options versus one short option, as seen in Examples 1 and 2. It is possible to use other ratios of long options versus short options.

Let's look at an example trade that uses a ratio of three long calls versus two short calls:

- **Example 3.** In October, ZYX is trading at $28.40. There seems to be a good possibility that ZXY is about to break out and will be at $40 within the next six months. Let's see how we might play this with a 3:2 backspread trade using April calls.

  Trade: Buy 3 Apr 32.5 calls at $.85 per share and sell 2 Apr 30 calls at $2.10 per share.

  Initial credit = $165 [2(2.1 × 100) − 3(.85 × 100) = 165].

  Max risk = $335.

See Figure 22-3 for a risk graph that depicts this trade.

This trade can be thought of as a combination of (1) one long Apr 32.5 call purchased for $85 [.85 × 100 = 85] and (2) two bear call spreads composed of two long Apr 32.5 calls and two short Apr 30 calls which generate a credit of $250 [2(2.1 − .85) × 100 = 250]. The credit more than pays for the long call, leaving a net credit of $165 on the combination.

The break-even point for this trade at expiration is ZYX at $35.85. At that point, the long call has a profit of $335 [(35.85 − 32.50) × 100 = 335]. This profit together with the initial credit of $165 exactly offsets the $500 cost of closing the two credit spreads [2(32.5 − 30.0) × 100 = 500].

Suppose that ZYX has risen to $40 as the April option's expiration date arrives. The net profit on the 3:2 call backspread is the profit that the unencumbered call makes above its break-even price of $35.85. In this

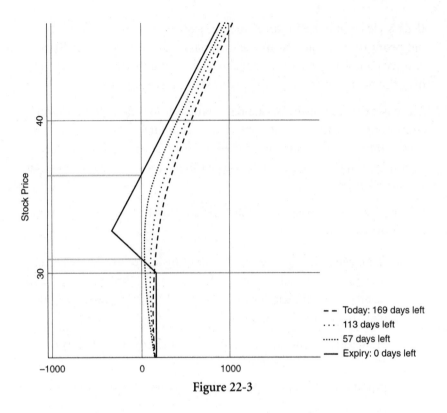

Figure 22-3

case, the profit would be $415 [(40.0 − 35.85) × 100 = 415]$. The return on this trade relative to maximum risk is 124 percent.

Comments

The backspread trade is cheap to initiate, possibly even providing an initial credit. In comparing the previous examples, note that to have an initial credit, the strike prices of the long and short options must be further apart.

These trades have unlimited potential to profit from large moves in the stock price. If the strike prices of the long and short options are far apart, a larger move in the stock price is required to produce a profit.

Unlike most spreads, the backspread trade can achieve a maximum profit if the big move in the stock price occurs before expiration.

The maximum loss in a backspread trade occurs at expiration when the stock price coincides with the strike price of the short option(s). This loss is always greater than the original debit to initiate the trade.

The backspread trade will require some margin in your brokerage account. The two legs of the trade that represent a credit spread will require margin equal to the difference in strike prices between the long and short options.

23

BUTTERFLY SPREADS

The *butterfly spread trade* is typically a cheap trade with low risk and lots of leverage. The drawback of the butterfly trade is that it focuses on a narrow range of profitability. The trade can be arranged to have a wider profit range, but then it becomes considerably more expensive.

These spreads can be used in various ways. The most common strategy utilizes a butterfly trade to target a strike price toward which a stock or index is trending. They can also be traded with adjustments, although this usually adds additional risk to the trade. Another version of the butterfly has an unbalanced form, so as to favor price movement in one direction.

Standard Butterfly Trade

Let's consider an example of the standard butterfly trade:

- **Example 1.** In early July, XYZ stock is trading at $30 per share. Your feeling is that over the next four to five months, this stock is going to move sideways. To focus on the $30 price with plenty of leverage, you initiate the following butterfly trade.

  Trade:

  Buy 1 Nov 25 call for $6.30 per share. Cost = 6.30 × 100 = $630.

  Sell 2 Nov 30 calls for $2.80 per share. Credit = 2.75 × 200 = $560.

  Buy 1 Nov 35 call for $.60 per share. Cost = .60 × 100 = $60.

  Net cost = $130 [630 + 60 – 560 = 130].

  Max risk = $130.

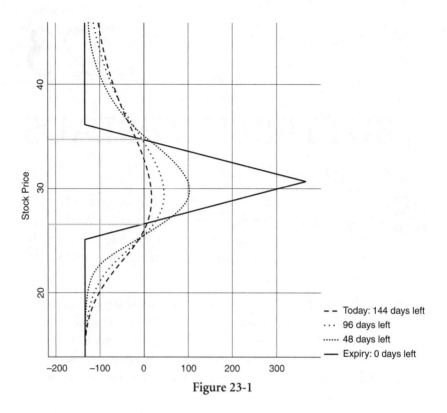

Figure 23-1

See Figure 23-1 for a risk graph that depicts this trade.

The butterfly trade derives its name from the appearance of its risk graph. This is best seen if the risk graph of Figure 23-1 is rotated clockwise through ninety degrees. Then the body of the butterfly lies in the V between $25 and $35. The top edges of the V are connected to the wings of the butterfly as represented by the straight portions of the risk graph that extend out from $25 and $35.

Another interpretation of this butterfly trade is a combination of a Nov 25 through Nov 30 bull call spread and a Nov 30 through Nov 35 bear call spread. The bull call spread has a net debit of $350 [630 − 280 = 350], whereas the bear call spread creates a net credit of $220 [280 − 60 = 220]. The combination then has a net cost of $130 [350 − 220 = 130].

As seen in Figure 23-1, the maximum return on the butterfly spread occurs if XYZ closes at exactly $30 on the November option's expiration date. In that case, the Nov 25 call can be sold for $500, while the other options all expire worthless. Thus, the net profit on the trade is $370 [500 − 130 = 370], which represents a 285 percent return on the initial investment. Options traders often refer to the price that maximizes the return from the butterfly spread as the *sweet spot*.

If XYZ closes below $30 at expiration, the net profit will be less because the Nov 25 call will be worth less than $500. If XYZ closes above $30, the 2 Nov 30 calls must be bought back to close the trade, which decreases the net return. The maximum loss of $130 occurs in the extreme cases when XYZ closes either below $25 or above $35 at expiration. The spread makes a profit whenever XYZ is between $26 and $34 at expiration.

Comments

Example 1 illustrates both the positive and negative features of the butterfly spread. The positive features are that (1) it is typically an inexpensive trade, and (2) its maximum return provides plenty of leverage. The negative features are that (1) the price range for a profit is rather narrow, and (2) to achieve the maximum return, the timing is critical because the stock price needs to be exactly at the sweet spot on the expiration date.

As an alternate approach to Example 1, puts could have been used rather than calls. That is, buy one Nov 35 put and one Nov 25 put, while selling two Nov 30 puts. The cost and results for this put butterfly would have been similar to those for the call butterfly, because the initial price of XYZ was at the sweet spot of both trades.

To target a sweet spot either above or below the current price of XYZ, you should examine both a call butterfly and a put butterfly to see which offers the cheaper price. The cost of a butterfly spread that has a sweet spot significantly far from the current stock price is usually going to be more expensive. Going out to a more distant expiration date will generally reduce the cost of the butterfly.

Butterfly Trade with Adjustments

Let's look at a different way of handling a butterfly spread that involves an adjustment that is made somewhat later in the trade. This approach will cater to a more volatile stock whose price tends to make dramatic swings between price extremes during the timeframe of a few months.

- **Example 2.** In early July, suppose XYZ is trading near $30, but there is an indication that it may be moving up in the near future. Set up a butterfly spread to initially focus on the $35 level.

  Trade:

  Buy 1 Nov 40 put for $9.90 per share. Cost = 9.90 × 100 = $990.

  Sell 2 Nov 35 puts for $4.60 per share. Credit = 4.60 × 200 = $920.

  Buy 1 Nov 30 put for $.80 per share. Cost = .80 × 100 = $80.

  Net credit = $150 [990 + 80 – 920 = 150].

  Max risk = $150.

See Figure 23-2 for a risk graph that depicts this trade.

Now let's examine a couple of scenarios to see how this trade might progress:

- The ideal scenario is for the price of XYZ to coincide with the sweet spot of $35 when the November options expire. In that case, the Nov 40 put could be sold for $500, while the other options all expire worthless. Thus, the net profit on the trade is $350 [500 – 150 = 350], which represents a 233 percent return on the initial cost.

- In another scenario that caters to more volatile price swings, suppose that XYZ has run up to $38 in late September and appears to have stalled at that level. The butterfly spread might show a slight profit, but it would be too small to warrant exiting the whole trade. However, the Nov 35 puts that were originally sold for $4.60 might now be worth only $1.

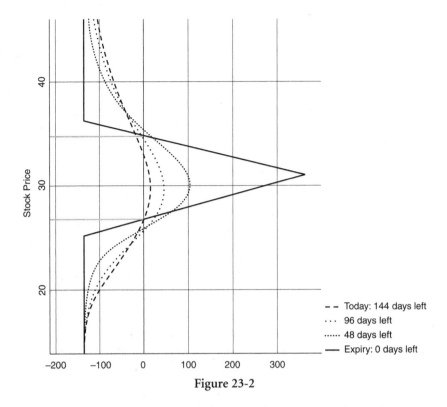

Figure 23-2

An adjustment that could be made here is to buy back the 2 Nov 35 puts to secure a $720 profit [920 − (1.0 × 200) = 720] on those options. This adjustment leaves you with the following residual position:

Long 1 Nov 40 put. Cost basis = $270 [990 − 720 = 270].

Long 1 Nov 30 put. Cost basis = $80.

Note: In this residual position, the $720 profit was applied to the cost of the Nov 40 put, but could have been applied in any convenient manner to the cost of the long puts.

The total cost basis of the residual position is $350 [270 + 80 = 350]. This means that we have taken on an extra $200 of risk beyond the original cost in an attempt to expand our profit range.

See Figure 23-3 for a risk graph that depicts the residual position.

This residual position has a great profit potential for any downside move in XYZ. Suppose XYZ falls to $31 in early November. The Nov 40

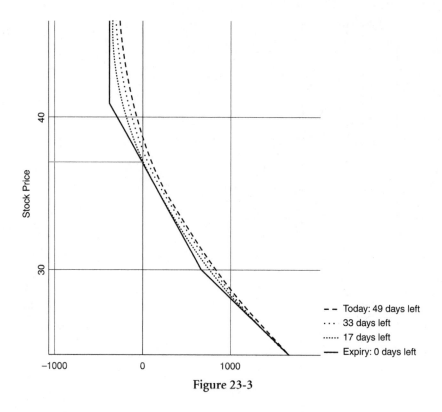

Figure 23-3

Legend:
- – – Today: 49 days left
- · · · 33 days left
- ······ 17 days left
- —— Expiry: 0 days left

Axis labels: Stock Price (vertical); values 40, 30. Horizontal axis: −1000, 0, 1000.

put might be worth \$9.20, and the Nov 30 put might be worth \$.50. Selling both options would bring in \$970 [(9.20 + .50) × 100 = 970] for a net profit of \$620 [970 − 350 = 620]. That represents a 177 percent gain based on the \$350 cost basis of the residual position.

Comment

A word of caution about the butterfly spread of Example 2. If XYZ fails to move up, the short Nov 35 puts are deep-in-the-money and will have lost most of their time value by early November. In this case, there is a danger of early assignment.

Unbalanced Butterfly Trade

Let's consider an example of an unbalanced butterfly trade:

- **Example 3.** In early July, the ZYX index is trading at \$150 per share. Your feeling is that, over the next two months, this index is going to move sideways with a slight bias toward also moving higher. To focus on the $150 price while also allowing for upward movement, you initiate an unbalanced butterfly trade.

Trade:

Buy 1 Aug 145 put for $1.40 per share. Cost = 1.40 × 100 = $140.

Sell 2 Aug 150 puts for $3.20 per share. Credit = 3.20 × 200 = $640.

Buy 1 Aug 152.50 put for $4.50 per share. Cost = 4.50 × 100 = $450.

Net credit = $50 [640 − 140 − 450 = 50].

Max risk = $200.

See Figure 23-4 for a risk graph that depicts this trade.

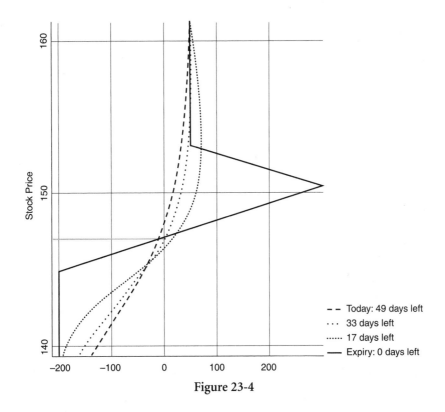

Figure 23-4

This trade is established for a small credit. If ZYX is above $152.50 at expiration, all the puts will expire worthless, and the credit becomes a profit. As seen in Figure 23-4, this credit gives the butterfly an unbalanced bias toward the upside.

As with a standard butterfly, the maximum return occurs if ZYX closes at the sweet spot of $150 on the August option's expiration date. In that case, the Aug $152.50 put can be sold for $250, while the other options all expire worthless. Thus, the net profit on the trade is $300 [250 + 50 = 300], which includes the initial credit.

The maximum loss of $200 occurs whenever ZYX closes below $145 at expiration. This unbalanced butterfly spread has a break-even point of $147 at expiration.

24

IRON CONDORS AND DOUBLE DIAGONALS

The *iron condor trade* and the *double diagonal trade* are popular nondirectional strategies. These trades are designed for a stock or index whose price is expected to remain within a reasonably narrow range during a one-to-two-month time period. Both of these trades are credit trades. That is, the initial result of doing the trade is that cash is brought into your brokerage account. With these credit trades, the plan becomes one of waiting for the time value of the short options to dissipate as the stock price moves in a generally sideways direction.

The Iron Condor Trade

The basic setup of the iron condor is to sell one out-of-the-money call and one out-of-the-money put with strike prices that are about equally placed from the middle of the price range of the stock. To hedge these short positions, buy one call and one put that are even further out-of-the-money. All of these options have the same expiration date. Because the purchase prices of the long options are less than the sale prices of the short options, the iron condor creates a net credit.

Another interpretation of an iron condor is a combination of two vertical credit spreads. A bull put spread is established with the short put strike price near the bottom of the price range of the stock. Additionally, a bear call spread is established with the short call strike price near the top of the price range of the stock. Both spreads have the same expiration date. The combined credit from both vertical spreads is the total credit for the iron condor.

The goal of the iron condor is to have both short options expire worthless and hence retain all of the initial credit received when the trade was initiated.

By using options that will expire in one to two months, the expectation is that the price of the stock will not have time to drift outside of its normal trading range. For the maximum return on the iron condor, the stock price at expiration needs to be between the strike prices of the short options.

Let's look at an example of an iron condor trade:

- **Example 1.** You observe that XYZ stock has recently been trading in a range of $50 to $60. In late December, the stock is at $56, and you decide to set up an iron condor trade using February options.

  Trade: Sell 1 Feb 60 call for $1.85 and sell 1 Feb 50 put for $1.10. Buy 1 Feb 65 call for $.70 and buy 1 Feb 45 put for $.40. This creates a net credit of $1.85 per share, thereby bringing $185 [(1.85 + 1.10 − .70 − .40) × 100 = 185] into your brokerage account.

See Figure 24-1 for a risk graph that depicts this trade.

As Figure 24-1 shows, the best-case scenario is for the price of XYZ to be between $50 and $60 at the February option's expiration. In this case, all the options expire worthless and the original credit of $185 is converted to profit.

The worst-case scenario arises if the price of XYZ is either below $45 or above $65. In either of these cases, one of the credit spreads must be closed for a cost of $5 per share. This results in a net loss on the trade of $315 [(5.0 × 100) − 185 = 315].

Typically, there is no need to allow the trade to progress to the stage of a worst-case scenario. As seen in Figure 24-1, reasonable exit points would be if the price of XYZ falls to $48 or rises to $62. In either of these cases, the trade could be exited for a loss of about $100.

There is a margin requirement on iron condor trades. Because the two vertical spreads that make up the iron condor are credit spreads, some

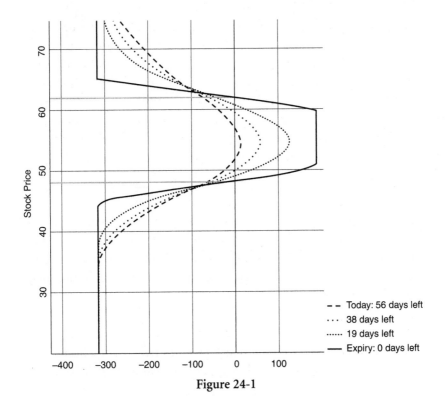

Figure 24-1

brokers will require margin on both. The more options-friendly brokers will only require margin on one of the vertical spreads in recognition of the fact that at least one of the two spreads must expire worthless.

The Double Diagonal Trade

The basic setup of the double diagonal is to sell one out-of-the-money call and one out-of-the-money put with strike prices that are about equally placed from the middle of the price range of the stock. These two short options have the same expiration date, usually one to two months until expiration. To hedge these short positions, buy one call and one put that are even further out-of-the-money, and with at least one additional month until expiration. Because the purchase prices of the long options are less than the sale prices of the short options, the double diagonal creates a net credit.

Another interpretation of the double diagonal is a combination of two diagonal calendar spreads. A diagonal calendar spread with puts is established with the short put strike price near the bottom of the price range of the stock. Another diagonal calendar spread with calls is established with the short call strike price near the top of the price range of the stock. Both of the short options have the same expiration date. Both of the long options have the same expiration date, usually one to two months later than the short options.

As with the iron condor, the goal of the double diagonal is to have both short options expire worthless. Assuming that the short options do expire worthless, you will have choices about how to handle the trade going forward. (1) One choice is to sell the long options for their residual value, even though they do not expire for at least one month. (2) Another choice is to sell new options, thereby creating either another double diagonal or an iron condor.

Let's look at an example of a double diagonal trade:

- **Example 2.** You observe that XYZ stock has recently been trading in a range of $50 to $60. In late December, the stock is at $56, and you decide to set up a double diagonal trade using February and March options.

  Trade: Sell 1 Feb 60 call for $1.85 and sell 1 Feb 50 put for $1.10. Buy 1 Mar 65 call for $1.20 and buy 1 Mar 45 put for $.70. This creates a net credit of $1.05 per share, thereby bringing $105 [(1.85 + 1.10 − 1.20 − .70) × 100 = 105] into your brokerage account.

See Figure 24-2 for a risk graph that depicts this trade.

As suggested by Figure 24-2, if XYZ is between $50 and $60 at the February expiration date, the short options will expire and the long options sold, leading to a profit of $150 to $180 on the trade.

The worst-case scenario arises if the price of XYZ is either below $35 or above $75. In either of these cases, Figure 24-2 suggests that the trade will be showing a loss of about $400.

As with the iron condor, there is typically no need to allow the double diagonal trade to progress to the stage of a worst-case scenario. As seen

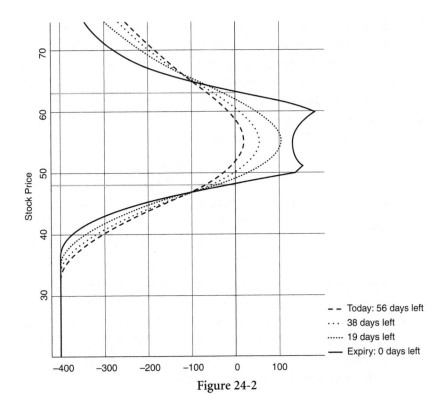

Figure 24-2

in Figure 24-2, reasonable exit points would be if the price of XYZ falls to $48 or rises to $63. In either of these cases, the trade could be exited for a loss of about $100.

The margin requirement for the double diagonal trade is essentially the same as for an iron condor trade. Some brokers require margin on both diagonal calendar spreads, whereas the more options-friendly brokers will only require margin on one spread.

Comments

The main advantage of the iron condor is its simplicity at expiration if the stock price is between the strike prices of the short options. All options expire worthless and the trade is automatically closed without the need for any action. No commissions are incurred.

The main advantage of the double diagonal is the flexibility it offers for adjustments. In Example 2, if the price of XYZ moves up toward the $60 strike price of the short call or down toward the $50 strike price of the short put, the short February option can be rolled out to a March option. Alternatively, the Feb 60 calls can be rolled up to the Feb 65 calls, or the Feb 50 puts can be rolled down to the Feb 45 puts; either of which creates a Feb–Mar calendar spread with no margin issue.

Another advantage of the double diagonal is the possibility of continuation into the next month. In Example 2, if XYZ is between $50 and $60 at the February expiration, you have achieved a profit, and the long March options become free positions that can be played for another month. For example, those long options could be used as the outside legs of an iron condor for March.

A disadvantage of the double diagonal is the decision process that must take place following the expiration of the short options. Some action is required to either (1) sell the long options or (2) initiate new short legs so as to extend the trade for another month. In either case, this necessarily involves some decision about obtaining the best prices. Also, there will be additional commission charges.

25

AN END-OF-YEAR
TAX STRATEGY

S uppose you own a stock that has made a nice gain during the year, but you are concerned about a substantial pullback near the end of the year. Of course, you are reluctant to sell your stock and take your profit before January 1, because of the tax implications. You would like to avoid having to pay tax on that nice profit when the next April 15 arrives.

The IRS regulations make it essentially impossible for you to install any kind of cost-free hedge of your stock profit that would defer a tax payment into the next year. There is, however, a way to use options to provide some degree of cost-free protection of your profit without creating a taxable transaction. This chapter demonstrates a strategy that offers some limited protection of your profit while postponing a tax payment and staying within the IRS guidelines.

Tax Code Restrictions

Several options strategies are available to provide a complete, cost-free hedge of your stock profit. Unfortunately, the IRS does not allow such strategies to be employed for the purpose of postponing a tax payment. The IRS refers to such disallowed hedges as *constructive sales.* There is no need to dwell on the complicated definition of what constitutes a constructive sale, because our concern here is in a useful strategy that is allowed.

The IRS does permit the use of the married put strategy (see Chapter 17, "Married Puts") to protect profit in a stock. This strategy has the drawback that it is not cost-free, and in fact can be quite expensive in some circumstances. The married put strategy involves buying a put option to protect the stock, which could result in a significant cost for the desired protection of a large stock holding. A cost-free strategy is preferable.

An ideal cost-free protection strategy is to sell a deep-in-the-money call against your stock position, but the IRS interprets this as one of the disallowed constructive sales. The IRS does permit selling an in-the-money call, but restricts just how deep in-the-money you can go. Those in-the-money calls that are allowed by the IRS are referred to as *qualified covered calls*. The strategy presented here shows how to achieve a reasonable level of profit protection by using qualified covered calls.

Qualified Covered Calls

Because our interest is to defer taking profit in the stock until the next year, it is assumed that any covered call will have an expiration date in January or later. For our purposes, we follow the IRS guidelines for a qualified covered call that is sold when there are at least 31 days before it expires, but not more than 90 days until it expires.

The basic IRS rule is that you can only drop down to the first strike price level below a certain specified stock price. The specified stock price is the closing price of the stock on the day before the covered call transaction is to be initiated, provided that the stock does not open more than 10 percent higher on the day planned for the transaction. If the stock does open more than 10 percent higher on the planned transaction day, you can only drop down to the first strike price level below the opening stock price.

The IRS guidelines also stipulate that, for stocks whose specified price is $150 or less, the strike price of the covered call cannot be more than $10 in-the-money when the trade is initiated. For stocks whose specified price is $25 or less, there is an additional restriction, namely that the strike price cannot be less than 85 percent of the specified stock price.

Basic Strategy

The goal here is to achieve a reasonable level of cost-free profit protection by selling a covered call that meets the IRS guidelines.

The benefit of selling a covered call is that the cash received serves to offset a pullback in the stock price. By selling an in-the-money call, more cash is received, which provides a bigger cushion in case the price of your stock begins to fall before the new year arrives. To create the largest cushion, you want to maximize the difference between the stock price and the strike price of the qualified covered call.

The cash received from the sale of the call does not become a taxable transaction until the option position is resolved by one of the following events: (1) option expires, (2) option is exercised, or (3) option is bought back to close the short position. Outcome 1 does not occur before the January expiration date. As a practical matter, it is unlikely that outcome 2 would happen until after January 1. There is no reason for outcome 3 because the owner of the stock controls that decision.

The first step of the basic strategy is to sell 1 January call for every 100 shares of stock you own. Typically, it is most convenient to use a January call so that an early resolution of the position can be made soon after January 1.

The selection of the strike price must comply with the IRS guidelines for a qualified covered call. On the day planned for selling the call, check to make sure that the stock opened no more than 10 percent higher than the previous day's close. After this is verified, the acceptable strike price for the covered call is the first one below the closing price of the previous day. If the stock did open more than 10 percent higher, the acceptable strike price for the covered call is the first one below the opening price of the stock.

The second step is to make sure that you are complying with the time constraints for initiating the covered trade. Because we are considering an end-of-year strategy, it is relatively easy to comply with the constraint of initiating the trade with no more than 90 days until expiration of the January call. As a rough guide, this implies that the covered call would be sold sometime after the October option's expiration date. To comply with the 31-day rule, the sale needs to take place no later than the December date that is 31 days from the January option's expiration date.

Keep in mind that you are not required to initiate the trade on any particular date, so long as you do not get within the 31 days until the January options expire. If you planned to do the trade on a certain day only to find that the stock price is unfavorable on that day, wait until a better opportunity presents itself.

If for some reason you were to decide to initiate this covered call strategy with less than 31 days until the January option's expiration date, you must consider selling a call that has a February or later expiration date.

Suppose that you have succeeded in initiating the covered call strategy. Let's examine the more likely outcomes. If the stock price is above the strike price at the January option's expiration date, your stock will be called away and sold at the strike price of the option. The sum of the cash received from selling the call option plus the proceeds from the stock sale at the strike price will usually exceed the price of the stock at the time you initiated the option trade. Of course, these transactions will have tax consequences for profit earned in the year that the stock is sold.

In some circumstances, you may decide to buy back the covered call after January 1, to be able to continue holding the stock without any concern that it might be called away from you. This may or may not be a wise investment decision, but it will nevertheless delay the tax consequences.

If the stock price has fallen below the strike price at expiration, you may still receive a return that exceeds the price of the stock at the time you initiated the options trade. Furthermore, if the stock price is below the strike price at expiration, the option will not be exercised and you can continue to hold your stock if that seems to be a desirable choice.

To illustrate the basic strategy, here are some examples:

- **Example 1.** You paid $3,300 to buy 100 shares of XYZ at $33 in August. In early December, XYZ is at $68. You would like to sell the stock to collect more than 100 percent profit, but you are reluctant to create such a substantial taxable event in the current year. Let's employ the covered call strategy described above:

Suppose the stock closes at $68 on December 5 and opens at $69 on December 6. The stock price opened less than 10 percent above the previous day's close, so $68 is the price that determines the strike price for the qualified covered call. Because it is more than 31 days before the January option's expiration date, the Jan 65 call can be sold without incurring a current year tax consequence on your stock profit.

Suppose that on December 6 you sell one Jan 65 call for $7 per share. This brings $700 into your brokerage account with no tax implications until the option is resolved. You have now established some protection of your profit in XYZ stock.

Note that this call option has $3 of time value included in its price [(65 + 7) – 69 = 3], which makes it highly unlikely that it would be exercised against you before that time value disappears.

If XYZ is above $65 at the January option's expiration date, your stock will be called away and sold for $65 per share, which brings another $6,500 into your brokerage account. Then you will have received a total of $7,200 [700 + 6,500 = 7,200], which represents a profit of $3,800 [7,200 – 3,400 = 3,800]. Note that this profit exceeds that which would have been received from selling the stock at $69. For tax purposes this profit is generated in the new year.

The break-even price for this covered call position is $62. If XYZ is at $62 at the January expiration, the short option expires worthless and the stock could be sold for $62 per share. Then you will have received a total of $6,900 [700 + 6200 = 6,900], which is exactly what you would have received if the stock had been sold at $69 on December 6. Earning the profit of $3,500 [6,900 – 3,400 = 3,500] would be a taxable transaction in the new year.

Note that if the price of XYZ is below $65 at the January option's expiration, it is not necessary that the stock be sold, which would avoid any tax on the gain in stock value. The $700 profit received from selling the Jan 65 call would be a taxable transaction in the new year.

- **Example 2.** Assume that the scenario is the same as Example 1, except that XYZ opens at $72 on December 6. This is still less than a 10 percent gain over the previous day's closing price, so the Jan 65 call is again the qualified covered call. The Jan 65 call might be sold for $8 or more per share, for an even greater cushion than in Example 1.

- **Example 3.** Assume that the scenario is the same as Example 1, except that XYZ opens at $75.50 on December 6. This is an 11 percent gain over the previous day's close. By the IRS rules, this raises the allowed strike level to the Jan 75 call. This is not the best opportunity to employ the covered call strategy, because the Jan 75 call might be priced at only about $1.50 per share, which does not provide much downside protection.

Follow-Up Variations

1. At any time before your stock is called away, you can elect to keep your stock by buying back the short call option. Of course, this could be costly if the stock price has risen significantly since you sold the option. Do not let greed overpower good judgment by deciding not to give up the stock for a price that was originally acceptable to you.

   On the other hand, if the stock price has gone down, you can buy back the short call for less than it was sold and make a profit on the option, while you continue to hold the stock for future gains. In this situation, avoid buying back the option before January, because the profit on the option transactions would be treated as a taxable gain in the current year.

2. In January, you might decide to "roll out" of the short call option and replace it with one that has a later expiration date. This postpones the need to give up your stock. Suppose the stock price has risen slightly and you decide that you

want to keep your stock. Then, buy back the January call option at a small loss and complete the rollout by selling another option from a later month with a strike price above the level of the current stock price. Your objective in this rollout maneuver is to bring in enough cash from selling the new option to offset the loss incurred from buying back the January option.

Comments

When looking for a favorable set up to employ this covered call strategy, watch for those days in which the stock closes with a price that is just below a strike. If the stock then opens higher the next day (but not more than 10 percent higher), this allows you to capture a large intrinsic value from the sale of the option in addition to its time value. This approach will provide the greatest protective cushion in case the stock price does begin to fall (see Example 2).

Make sure that the covered call has some time value included in its price. This guards against an early exercise that would require you to sell your stock before January 1.

It should be noted that after the trade is initiated, the maximum return from the stock has been capped. Further increases in the stock price will not provide any more profit.

Consult your professional tax adviser before implementing the strategy described here to determine its suitability for your individual circumstances.

Section III

SPECIAL TOPICS

Section III includes Chapters 26 through 30. Each chapter in this section covers a topic that is intended for people with options experience who want to develop a broader background. All of these chapters are marked with an asterisk, so this whole section can be passed over by beginners during their first reading of this book.

26*

DAY TRADING AN INDEX WITH OPTIONS

I f you are ready to try your hand at day trading an index using options, here is an overview of how to get started. Some ideas will be included on what index to use as well as the basic tools you will need to pursue this endeavor.

A large number of indexes have options. For day trading purposes, you want an index with highly liquid options, and you want an index with a range of daily price movement that is sufficient to create opportunities for profit. A favorite index of many traders that meets these criteria is the S&P 100, better known as the OEX.

The OEX has an average daily price range of about 4 points. Seldom is the daily price range less than 2 points, and during every month you can expect to see several days with a price range of 7 to 8 points. Days with a price range of 10 points or more are relatively infrequent. An OEX price movement of 5 to 6 points is typically accompanied by a Dow price movement of about 100 points.

The most conservative way to day trade the OEX is simply to buy a call or a put, depending on which way you anticipate the index price to move. The recommended option is the front-month, slightly out-of-the-money call or put. Depending on how close it is to the expiration date, the price of this option will be in the range of $2 to $7. The magnitude of the delta of this option typically is about 0.40 to 0.50. Keep in mind that as the index price moves in the desired direction, the magnitude of the delta of the option will increase, thereby improving your potential for profit.

A reasonable goal is to capture about 60 percent of the price movement of the index for the day. On a typical day when there is a 4-point price movement in the OEX, you are looking to participate in a movement of about 2.5 points. With a delta of .40, this suggests that you are looking for a $1 per share gain in the price of the option; however, with slippage, the gain is more likely to be about $.80 to $.90 per share. If you are trading 10 contracts, this translates to a profit of $800 to $900. Commissions will diminish that profit by $50 or less.

Ideally, you would like to limit the average loss on your losing trades to less than the average profit on your winning trades. Realistically, this is difficult to achieve. If you set your stops too tight in an effort to restrict loss, you will be prematurely taken out of many trades that would ultimately become profitable. For the typical 4-point price movement in the OEX, a good goal is to hold the loss on your losing 10 contract trades to $1,000, including commissions.

Based on the average profit and loss per trade suggested previously, you will need to have at least two winning trades for every losing trade to make day trading the OEX a worthwhile venture. For every three trades involving a 4-point move in the OEX, you need two winners for a profit of $1,500 [2 × (800 − 50) = 1,500] to offset one loser with a loss of $1,000. That produces a net gain of $500 on the three trades.

This projected return of $500 on every three trades based on a 10 contract trade can be adjusted to suit your tolerance for risk by using a different number of contracts. Using a different lot size does bring some other issues into consideration. With fewer contracts, there is the advantage of quicker and better fills on your trades, but the disadvantage that commissions represent a larger percentage of the trade. With significantly more contracts, some liquidity may be lost, but the effect of commissions will be diminished. On those days where the price range is significantly more or less than the typical 4 points, the expected profits and losses on the trades must be appropriately scaled.

It should be emphasized that "day trading" means that you are not going to hold any position overnight. Of course, you can decide that you want to hold a position overnight or even for several days, but then you are into a whole new philosophy of trading. If you do decide to hold a position overnight, be aware that you are vulnerable to substantially more risk.

The most important element in the day trading approach described previously is achieving the 2:1 ratio of winning trades to losing trades. Accomplishing this goal will depend on your skill in reading market direction, as well as your skill at entering and exiting trades. Developing these skills will require time and practice.

Some basic tools can prove useful in helping you to develop the necessary skills for day trading. First of all, you need a trading platform that enables you to view all the important data in real time. You must be able to simultaneously view the option price and the index price in real time. The trading platform must also enable you to quickly issue an order to either enter or exit a trade. In day trading, it is imperative that you are able to see what is happening in real time and be able to act swiftly on your observations.

Your visualization of the index price movement should be in the form of a chart. It is best if you can follow the index price movement on at least two charts whose bars are based on different time frames. A common choice is one chart with 1-minute bars and another chart with 10-minute bars. The 1-minute bar chart is useful in deciding on precise entry and exit points, whereas the 10-minute bar chart helps you to recognize general trends in the price movement of the index.

Your charts should be supplemented with some technical indicators that will assist you in determining a trend in the index price. While gaining experience, you can experiment with a variety of technical indicators, but almost all day traders use some type of stochastic oscillator in their analysis of short-term market movement.

Probably the most common stochastic oscillator is the (14,3,3) slow stochastic. This is the default setting on many data services that offer stochastic analysis. You should set up this oscillator on both your 1-minute bar chart and your 10-minute bar chart. Loosely speaking, the stochastic oscillator is used to indicate when a sustained trend in one direction (up or down) is likely to reverse and go the other way. The day trader uses these indications of a change in direction as potential entry and exit points for trading. The most reliable indications occur when the stochastics of both the 1-minute and 10-minute charts agree on a change in price direction.

Even though you may be day trading the OEX, it is wise to always be aware of the general trend in the market on a longer time frame. For example, if the market is in a strong bullish trend, you should give some preference to bullish day trades in the OEX. Keep in mind that favorite cliché of traders—"the trend is your friend." During periods when the market is choppy, day trading can be particularly challenging because you are more likely to react to a false signal of market direction.

The discussion here is not sufficient for you to immediately step into the role of a successful OEX day trader, but it should be useful in getting you started in the right direction. It is highly recommended that you begin by practice trading and keeping a journal of your "paper trades." This will help you to get a feel for how the option price reacts in response to changes in the index price. You also want to become comfortable with reading the signals provided by the stochastic oscillator before you attempt any real trades.

Comments

Day trading is not for everyone. It requires lots of discipline and a personality that can handle the rollercoaster of emotions that come from watching minute-by-minute market movement.

If you plan to do some day trading, check with your broker about requirements for your account. The basic requirement of all brokers is that you maintain an account balance of $25,000, but some brokers may have additional restrictions.

27*

DELTA-NEUTRAL TRADING

Delta-neutral trading can take on a variety of different forms and encompasses much more material than can be covered in this one chapter. There are delta-neutral strategies designed to generate profits, as well as delta-neutral strategies designed to protect profits. In this chapter, the basic concept of delta-neutral portfolios is discussed, and an example is used to demonstrate how trading a delta-neutral position can generate profits.

Before discussing delta-neutral trading, it is worthwhile to review the concept of the "delta" of a financial instrument (stock, option, future, and so on). Extending the definition stated in Chapter 4, "The Greeks," the delta of a financial instrument is the change in value of that instrument when the price of the underlying stock (or index) increases by $1, while all other influences are held fixed. The delta can be either positive or negative depending on whether the value of the financial instrument increases or decreases in response to a $1 increase in the stock price.

To review the concept of the delta, let's see how it applies to some simple stock and options positions:

- As an almost trivial case, suppose the financial instrument is that of being long one share of XYZ stock. If the price of XYZ increases by $1, the long position of one share increases in value by $1 and hence the delta = 1.00 [1.00/1.00 = 1.00]. Likewise, if the financial instrument is that of being long 100 shares of XYZ and the price of XYZ increases by $1, the value of the long position increases by $100, and hence the delta = 100 [100/1.00 = 100].

- Suppose that the financial instrument is that of being short one share of XYZ stock. If the price of XYZ increases by $1, the short position of one share decreases in value by $1 and hence the delta = −1.00 [−1.00/1.00 = −1.00]. Likewise, if the financial instrument is being short 100 shares of XYZ and the price of XYZ increases by $1, the value of the short position decreases by $100, and hence the delta = −100 [−100/1.00 = −100].

Let's also look at the delta of those cases where the financial instrument is an at-the-money option on XYZ. In each case, we assume that the price of XYZ stock is initially at $30.

The price of an at-the-money call option will typically increase by $.50 when the price of the stock increases by $1, and hence it has a delta = .50 on a per-share basis. So, if the $30 call has a price of $2, and XYZ stock goes up to $31, the price of the $30 call should increase to $2.50 [2.00 + (.50 × 1.00) = 2.50]. Because 1 call contract represents 100 shares of stock, it follows that 1 long at-the-money call has a total delta = 50 [.50 × 100 = 50].

For a short $30 call, the position has a delta = −.50 on a per-share basis. Accounting for 100 shares of stock in the contract, the position of being short one at-the-money call has a total delta = −50 [−.50 × 100 = −50].

The price of an at-the-money put option will typically decrease by $.50 when the price of the stock increases by $1. So, if the $30 put has a price of $1.75, and XYZ goes up to $31, the price of the $30 put should decrease to $1.25 [1.75 + (−.50 × 1.00) = 1.25]. Because 1 put contract represents 100 shares of stock, it follows that one long at-the-money put has a total delta = −50 [−.50 × 100 = −50].

For a short $30 put, the position has a delta = .50 on a per-share basis. Accounting for 100 shares of stock in the contract, the position of being short one at-the-money call has a total delta = 50 [.50 × 100 = 50].

When the strike price of the call or put option is deeper in-the-money, the magnitude of the delta increases. Analogously, when the strike price is further out-of-the-money, the magnitude of the delta decreases. For example, a long XYZ $25 call might have a delta = .75, whereas a long XYZ $40 call might have a delta = .25. Likewise, a long XYZ $35 put might have a delta = −.75, whereas a long XYZ $20 put might have a delta = −.25.

In the preceding discussion, values of the delta have been suggested that are fairly typical of the various at-the-money, in-the-money, and out-of-the-money options. The actual values of the deltas change continuously as the stock price changes. These actual values are determined from the Black-Scholes model for pricing options. A good market data feed service will provide accurate values of the deltas for options in real time.

Now let's turn our attention to the general concept of a delta-neutral position for a portfolio that involves a combination of financial instruments. The definition of a *delta-neutral portfolio* is that the net delta of all the components of the portfolio is zero. Why is this significant?

The significance of a delta-neutral portfolio is that a small change in the price of the underlying stock will have essentially no effect on the net value of the portfolio. In other words, a delta-neutral portfolio is insensitive to small changes in the value of the stock that governs its components.

To illustrate the concept of a delta-neutral portfolio, consider one that is long 100 shares of XYZ stock at $30 and also long 2 XYZ $30 puts with a price of $1.75 per share. The long stock represents a delta = 100 [1.00 × 100 = 100], while the long puts represent a delta = −100 [2 × (−.50 × 100) = −100]. For the portfolio as a whole, the net delta is zero [100 − 100 = 0]. The total value of this portfolio is $3,350 [(100 × 30) + (200 × 1.75) = 3,350].

See Figure 27-1 for a risk graph that depicts this portfolio.

Let's see how the value of the preceding portfolio is insensitive to a modest decrease in the stock price. Suppose the price of XYZ falls to $29, which then reduces the value of the stock to $2,900. Because each long put has a delta = −.50 per share, a decrease in the stock price of $1 will increase the value to $2.25 per share [1.75 + ((−.50) × (−1.0)) = 2.25]. Thus, the total value of the two puts increases to $450 [2 × (100 × 2.25) = 450]. So, after a decrease of $1 in the stock price, the puts increase in value in a manner that maintains the portfolio value at $3,350 [2,900 + 450 = 3,350].

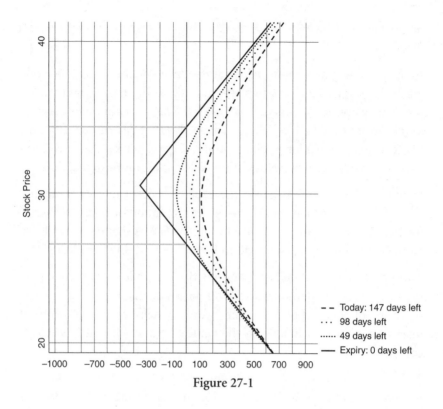

Figure 27-1

If instead the price of XYZ stock increased to $31, the value of the portfolio would again maintain the value of $3,350. In this case, the value of the stock would increase to $3,100, but the value of the two puts would be reduced to $250.

The delta-neutral effect is seen in the risk graph of Figure 27-1. Note that the short-term profit/loss curve is flat for stock prices near $30.

If the stock price undergoes larger changes (up or down), the net delta of the preceding portfolio would not remain near zero. Some adjustment would be required to return the portfolio to a delta-neutral status. Such adjustments can be employed as part of a trading strategy to generate profits from a delta-neutral portfolio.

Let's see how to use a delta-neutral trading strategy to produce profits from the preceding portfolio that is long 100 shares of XYZ stock at $30 and long 2 XYZ $30 puts with a price of $1.75 per share. For this strategy to be most effective, we need for the price of XYZ to swing back and forth in a price range centered around $30.

To begin, suppose fairly soon after the portfolio is set up, the price of XYZ drops to $25. The stock will have lost value, while the put options will have gained in value. The net value of the portfolio might even have increased, but not enough to justify cashing out for a profit. The puts are now sufficiently in-the-money for them to have a delta = −.75 per share and thus the two put contacts represent a total delta = −150 [2 × (−.75 × 100) = 150]. Because the long stock has a delta = 100, the whole portfolio has a delta = −50 [100 − 150 = −50].

To bring the portfolio back to a delta-neutral status, we can buy an additional 50 shares of stock at $25 per share. Then, with a portfolio that is long 150 shares of XYZ and long 2 XYZ $30 puts, the net delta is zero [150 − 150 = 0].

Now move forward in time and suppose the price of XYZ goes up to $31. The puts would return to a status of delta = −.50 per share and for the two contacts the total delta = −100. With the portfolio now having 150 shares of XYZ, the net delta = 50 [150 − 50 = 50].

To bring the portfolio back to a delta-neutral status, we can now sell the 50 shares of stock that were purchased at $25. This generates a profit of $300 [50 × (31 − 25) = 300].

Now suppose the price of XYZ continues up to $35. The $30 puts would then have a delta = −.25 per share and for the two contracts the total delta = −50. For the portfolio, the net delta = 50 [100 − 50 = 50].

To bring the portfolio back to a delta-neutral status, we can buy one XYZ $35 put for $2 per share and hence a total cost of $200. Because this new long put is at-the-money, it would have a delta = −.50 per share, and thus for one contract have a total delta = −50. Then, with a portfolio that is long 100 shares of XYZ, long 2 $30 puts and long 1 $35 put, the net delta is 0 [100 + {2 × (−25)} + {1 × (−50)} = 0].

Finally, as time continues to evolve, suppose the price of XYZ drops to $30. The $30 puts would again have a delta = −.50 per share, and for the two contracts the total delta = −100. The $35 put would have a delta = –.75, and for the one contract the total delta = –75. For the portfolio, the net delta = –75 [100 + {2 × (–50)} + {1 × (–.75) } = –75].

To bring the portfolio back to delta-neutral status, we can now sell the $35 put, which originally cost $2 per share, but now has a price of $6 per share. This generates a profit of $400 [100 × (6.0 – 2.0) = 400].

To summarize the results of this delta-neutral trading strategy, we see that a total profit of $700 [300 + $400 = 700] was generated by the adjustments that keep returning the portfolio to a status of zero net delta.

This example of delta-neutral trading was idealized to illustrate how the process is intended to work. In reality, it may be considerably more difficult to achieve these results. One issue not addressed here is the loss of time value in the options. This loss will offset some of the gains generated by the delta-neutral adjustments. A related issue is having the desired cycle of stock price movement occur within the lifetime of the options.

There are many other portfolios (combinations of options or stock and options) that enjoy a delta-neutral status, but which may be much less suitable for trading to maintain the neutral condition. For example, the iron condor trades discussed in Chapter 24, "Iron Condors and Double Diagonals," start out as delta-neutral, but can be difficult to continually adjust so as to maintain that status.

28*

THEORY OF
MAXIMUM PAIN

A lot of mystery surrounds the *theory of maximum pain*. This theory, more familiarly known as *max pain* or *strike price pegging*, attempts to explain the curious price movement of a stock (or index) that is sometimes observed during the last few days leading up to an option's expiration date.

Briefly, max pain refers to the situation in which the price of a stock seems to lock in on an option strike price as expiration nears. During the last few days, the stock price will vacillate around the strike price as if tethered by an elastic cord. The targeted strike price is typically the one that has the largest amount of open interest in the about-to-expire options.

A variety of explanations have been offered for the max pain effect. Some explanations describe a grand conspiracy on the part of the market makers to manipulate the stock price. It is suggested that the market makers collectively agree to steer the stock price to a level that would cause the largest number of at-the-money options to expire worthless. This explanation further assumes that it will be the retail traders left holding all of those worthless options at expiration, and hence the market makers exert the *maximum financial pain* on the investing public. This interpretation appears to be the source of the name for the max pain effect.

Because the max pain effect does seems to focus on a strike price, elaborate systems have been devised to predict an exact target price (somewhere near a strike price) at expiration. These predictions are based on algorithms that account for the amount of open interest associated with each of the front-month options. There are fee-based services that will provide these predicted target prices on any stock or index. Suffice to say that these predictions are frequently inaccurate.

Every month, as the option's expiration date draws near, you will find some stocks that exhibit fluctuations consistent with the max pain concept. But, there will be other stocks, apparently motivated by similar circumstances, where the price action is decidedly not like that suggested by max pain.

There has yet to be found a reliable theory that can consistently predict when the max pain effect will be observed and what price will be targeted. There is, however, a rational explanation as to what is happening when the max pain effect is observed. And this explanation does not require any grand conspiracy of the market makers. It only requires that some market makers take individual actions consistent with a logical, low-risk strategy to exploit the special circumstances that prevail as options expire.

It should be clear that the max pain effect will always be overridden by any breaking news that alters the fundamental outlook for a stock. If a company releases an earnings warning during options expiration week, it will be difficult to target a strike price while every major institution is dumping huge volumes of the stock.

Let's consider a more reasonable scenario to understand the market dynamics that produce the max pain effect without the need for any conspiracy. Suppose that XYZ is trading at $26 a few days before the expiration date of the front-month options. Also, suppose that there is a fairly high level of open interest in the about-to-expire calls and puts with a $25 strike price.

If the price of XYZ dips to $25.50, those retail traders who are long the front-month $25 calls will sense that time is working against them and be inclined to quickly sell their options to salvage some portion of their original investment. The market maker, who is well aware that the option owner is running out of time, will post a discounted bid price of only $.45 per share for the about-to-expire $25 call option.

The retail trader sells his option to the market maker for $.45 per share. Now the market maker is long the $25 call with a short lifetime. To protect himself, the market maker shorts 100 shares of XYZ at $25.50. This combination places him in a no-lose position with the potential for a windfall profit.

If the stock has gone up in price as expiration is reached, the market maker's short position in the stock will have lost money. But, he can exercise his long call to buy 100 shares of stock at $25 per share and cover his short stock position. In fact, there will be a profit of $5 per contract [(25.50 − 25 − .45) × 100 = 5], which may seem miniscule until you multiply that $5 by the hundreds of contracts handled by the market maker.

A windfall profit for the market maker occurs if XYZ incurs a significant drop in price. Suppose that XYZ has fallen to $24 at expiration. The market maker loses all of the $.45 per share that he paid for the long call, which expires worthless. On the other hand, he makes a profit of $1.50 per share on his short stock position, for a nice net profit of $105 per contract [(25.50 − 24 − .45) × 100 = 105].

What does this have to do with max pain? When the market maker shorts XYZ stock, a downward pressure is exerted on the stock price. If there is a large open interest in the $25 calls, the market maker could be shorting a large amount of stock. This action will tend to force the price of XYZ toward and possibly below $25.

Now let's turn our attention to another market maker who sees the price of XYZ fall to $24.50. He posts a discounted bid price of $.45 per share for the about-to-expire $25 puts. Those retail traders who are long these $25 puts rush to sell their options to salvage some portion of their original investment.

As soon as the market maker buys the put, he also buys 100 shares of XYZ stock at $24.50. As before, this combination places him in a no-lose position with the potential for a windfall profit.

If the stock has gone down in price as expiration is reached, the market maker's long position in the stock will have lost money. But he can exercise his long put and force someone to buy his 100 shares of stock at $25 per share. Again, this produces a profit of $5 per contract, which can add up to a tidy sum if it is repeated over hundreds of contracts handled by the market maker.

A windfall profit for this market maker occurs if XYZ makes a significant gain in price. Suppose that XYZ has risen to $26 at expiration. The market maker loses all of the $.45 per share that he paid for the long put, which expires worthless. On the other hand, he makes a profit of $1.50 per share on his long stock position for a nice net profit of $105 per contract.

This market maker also contributes to the max pain effect by buying XYZ stock, which exerts an upward pressure on the stock price. If there is a large open interest in the $25 puts, the market maker could be buying a large amount of stock. This action will tend to force the price of XYZ toward and possibly above $25.

Now we see that these two market makers, while acting independently, are actually working against each other in a dynamical manner that will tend to keep the stock price of XYZ close to $25. If there are large and roughly equal open interest numbers for both the $25 puts and $25 calls, this can lead to a high volume of buying and selling stock around the $25 level. The result of this back and forth action is a stock price that fluctuates around $25.

The previously described low-risk strategy used by the market makers during expiration week can also be employed by sophisticated retail traders. The retail trader will not be able to create a no-lose position, because he will not be able to buy the option at the discounted bid price. Instead, he will have to buy the option near the ask price, which will include some time value. If the trader is skillful in simultaneously buying the option and entering the corresponding stock position, the risk is limited to the time value in the option. Once established, this low-risk position has the potential for a windfall profit when the stock price moves in the right direction.

29*

IMPLIED VOLATILITY AND THE BLACK-SCHOLES FORMULA

The concept of implied volatility (IV) is important in evaluating an options trade. Experienced options traders have learned to appreciate that the implied volatility of an option suggests whether the option is overpriced or underpriced. To fully understand the meaning of implied volatility, you need some basic knowledge of the theory of options pricing, as expressed in the famous *Black-Scholes formula*.

The goal of this chapter is to provide some background and insight into the Black-Scholes formula and how IV is determined from that formula. Also, the use of IV data in trading is briefly discussed.

Historical Background

Back in the early 1970s when options on U.S. stocks were first introduced, everyone was guessing as to how they should be priced. Clearly, the option price should be related to the underlying stock price, but beyond that things were vague. At the time, there were three men on the forefront of theoretical finance trying to solve this problem, namely Fischer Black, Myron Scholes, and Robert Merton.

The work of these men led to an important formula for the pricing of options. This result became known as the Black-Scholes formula, because it first appeared in a 1973 paper authored by Black and Scholes.

Twenty-four years later, in 1997, Merton and Scholes were awarded the Nobel Prize in Economics for their groundbreaking work on the pricing of options. If Black had not passed away, he would have shared in the award.

Derivation of the Black-Scholes Formula

This section is intended to provide an overview of how the Black-Scholes formula is derived without presenting any of the mathematical details. Those readers who find this discussion a bit too technical can skip to the next section.

- **Part 1.** The first part of the theory is the development of an equation to describe the movement of stock prices. The equation contains two fundamental components that contribute to the change in the price of a stock. One component represents a simple return on your investment, which is proportional to the price of the stock. This component is something like compound interest earned on the money invested in buying the stock, and it always acts to increase the stock price. The other component is the random influence arising from minute-by-minute news, rumors, and spurious actions that create interest or disinterest in owning the stock. This random component can either positively affect the price change (due to good news), or negatively affect the price change (due to bad news). When a stock price drops, it is because the random component is sufficiently negative to overwhelm the simple return component.

  The sensitivity of the random component to minute-by-minute events is measured by a parameter called the *volatility*. This volatility parameter is different for each stock. For example, a recently released IPO stock often exhibits high volatility as it moves up or down 30 percent in reaction to a minor news item. Contrast this with the low volatility nature of a staid Dow stock that moves up or down only 3 percent on what appears to be important news. More about this volatility parameter will follow later.

- **Part 2.** The second part of the theory represents the essential contribution of Black, Scholes, and Merton. They proposed an idealized portfolio that is long several shares of stock and short one call option. The objective in this hypothetical portfolio is to continually adjust the number of shares of stock so as to counteract the random influence component described in Part 1. This requires an ongoing, second-by-second buying and selling of stock, which could only be achieved in an idealized setting.

  Next, it is reasoned that if this idealized portfolio is continually adjusted so as to be independent of random influences, it is guaranteed to earn a profit. In an efficient U.S. market, the best guaranteed profit is derived from a U.S. treasury bill or similar instrument whose return is based on the interest rate set by the Fed. The important conclusion to this reasoning is that the short-term increase in the value of the idealized portfolio must be exactly the same as the return from a U.S. treasury bill held over the same period of time.

- **Part 3.** In the final stage of the theory, the elements described in Parts 1 and 2 are linked together mathematically. Then, through the application of stochastic calculus (an extension of classical calculus that accounts for random effects), there emerges a partial differential equation that governs the price of the call option in the idealized portfolio. Solving that partial differential equation yields the "Black-Scholes formula" for calculating the price of a call option.

Application of the Black-Scholes Formula

Now let's discuss how the Black-Scholes formula might be used. The formula is a complicated mathematical expression and is not shown here. It is not essential to see the formula to appreciate how it is used. To actually calculate something from the formula requires using one of the many special calculators or software programs that has the formula programmed into its operation.

To calculate the current price of a call option, the Black-Scholes formula requires the input of five pieces of information, namely (1) the current price of the stock, (2) the strike price of the option, (3) the amount of time remaining until the option expires, (4) the current interest rate, and (5) the value of the volatility parameter for the stock, as described previously in Part 1.

Each of the required pieces of information is readily available, *except* for the value of the volatility parameter. There have been a multitude of ideas proposed as to how the value of this volatility parameter should be determined.

One possible choice for the value of the volatility parameter is the "historical volatility" associated with the stock. The historical volatility of a stock is calculated as the annualized standard deviation of the daily closing stock price relative to a mean value.

Using the value of historical volatility along with the other four pieces of input information, the Black-Scholes formula (via an options calculator) will provide a theoretical price for the option. As might be expected, the theoretically predicted price obtained by this calculation rarely agrees with the actual option price observed in the marketplace. This suggests that historical volatility is not the appropriate volatility parameter to accurately determine the price of an option.

Even though there is a disagreement between the actual option price and that predicted by the Black-Scholes formula using historical volatility of the stock, this discrepancy can be viewed as useful information. If we think of the predicted price as some sort of normal value based on an annualized average volatility, the actual price of the option can be viewed as either expensive or cheap by comparison. When the actual option price appears to be undervalued, we may want to buy it. If it appears to be overvalued, we may want to structure a trade in which that option is sold.

Implied Volatility

The application of the Black-Scholes formula as described in the last section is not the modern way in which it is used. As pointed out, the weak link in applying the formula is the choice of the volatility parameter.

To circumvent this issue, a different way to apply the formula was devised in which the volatility parameter was given a new interpretation.

Rather than trying to guess what value to use for the volatility parameter, the modern approach is to insert the actual option price from the marketplace into the Black-Scholes formula, and then let the formula tell us what the volatility should be. The value of the volatility parameter determined in this manner is called the *implied volatility,* or IV for short.

A major drawback in using the historical volatility to calculate theoretical options prices is that the same parameter value is used for all strike prices and all expiration months. In the modern approach of inserting actual option prices into the Black-Scholes formula, it is possible to calculate an IV for each individual option. These calculations reveal that the IV is generally quite different for each option. Also, the value of the IV can change quickly in response to changing circumstances surrounding the stock.

Applications of Implied Volatility

How is this IV used in trading? To begin with, we can compare the IV figure to the historical volatility. Also, we can examine the history of the IV itself to see how its current value differs from its values in the past. These comparisons will suggest if the option is currently overpriced or underpriced.

As a trading tool, IV proves particularly useful in selecting calendar spreads. To evaluate a possible calendar spread trade, compare the IV of two call (or put) options that have the same strike price but different expiration months. If the front-month option has a higher IV than the distant month, this is called a *volatility skew.* Such skews are important in initiating a calendar spread by buying the relatively cheap distant month option and selling the relatively expensive front-month option. This concept is discussed more fully in Chapter 13, "Advanced Calendar Spreads."

Checking the IV of an option is also a good way to avoid a trap, which is known in options trading as the *volatility crush.* Buying an option with an extremely high IV can be a costly mistake. High IV is often associated with some intense excitement about the underlying stock, such as the rumor of a buyout, FDA drug approval, settlement of a court case, and so on. As soon as the excitement is over, the IV falls back to some more normal level, and the value of the option is "crushed." An option purchased when its IV is high will be reduced to a fraction of its purchase price when the IV suddenly reverts to its mean value.

Comments

The Black-Scholes formula, and some modern variations of the formula, continue to play an important role in guiding options traders. It may seem backward to use the Black-Scholes formula to determine the IV of an option rather than to determine the theoretical price of an option. But, experience has shown that the IV of an option is a useful concept, because the prices in the marketplace are providing the true value of the volatility parameter for each individual option. Comparison of the current IV against historical norms leads to a more reliable estimation of whether an option is currently overpriced or underpriced.

The brokerage firms that are options friendly will provide IV values in their data feed. Also, the CBOE Web site offers a service that provides volatility data.

30*

THE PUT-CALL PARITY
RELATIONSHIP

Calls Cost More Than Puts

It is easy to verify that calls are actually more expensive than puts by making the following observation: Find a stock whose price coincides with a strike price. Then check the prices of the call and put options associated with that same strike price and which have the same expiration month. You might guess that these options would have the same price, but instead you would find that the price of the call is always greater than that of the put. The difference would be small in the front-month options, but becomes significantly larger as you go out to more distant expiration dates. The most pronounced difference in price is seen in the LEAPS options.

This price difference between puts and calls is known in option pricing theory as *put-call parity*, even though it might seem more appropriately titled as put-call disparity. What is the reason for this price difference and why is it important in options trading? This chapter discusses the answers to these questions.

To understand why calls are more expensive than puts, we need to delve just a bit into the theory of options pricing. A method frequently employed in the theoretical investigations of options is the use of hypothetical portfolios. The idea is to formulate an idealized portfolio, which can be compared against a more realistic portfolio in order to reveal some fundamental truth.

Let's consider a hypothetical portfolio that is long 100 shares of stock with a price per share denoted by S(t). This portfolio will also include one long put contract with a price per share denoted by P(t). The final component of this portfolio will be one short call contract with a price per share denoted by C(t).

Both options have the same strike price, K, and the same expiration date. The per-share value of the total portfolio is denoted by V(t). It can be expressed as follows:

$$V(t) = S(t) + P(t) - C(t). \quad [1]$$

Note that the letters used to designate various prices have been augmented with a (t) notation. This notation is used in mathematics to remind us that the value of each price can change as time progresses. The strike price K does not carry this notation because its value does not change with time.

In this idealized portfolio, we want to rule out the possibility that either of the options is exercised. So, we assume that both options retain enough time value to avoid any assignment before the expiration date.

To gain some insight into the nature of the idealized portfolio of [1], let's see what its value will be when the expiration date of the options is reached. We signify that the expiration time has arrived by denoting t = T. At expiration, the stock price S(T) could be either higher or lower than the strike price K of the options. We need to examine both possibilities.

If the stock price at expiration S(T) exceeds the strike price K, the call option will have a value of C(T) = S(T) − K, while the put option will be worthless, implying that P(T) = 0. In this case, it follows from [1] that V(T) = K. This says that the value of the idealized portfolio at expiration will be equal to the dollar value of the option strike price K.

If the stock price at expiration S(T) is less than the strike price K, the put option will have a value of P(T) = K − S(T), while the call option will be worthless, implying that C(T) = 0. In this case, it follows from [1] that V(T) = K. Again, we find that the value of the idealized portfolio at expiration is equal to the dollar value of the option strike price K.

After having examined both possible outcomes, we conclude that regardless of the price of the stock at the expiration date, this idealized portfolio described by [1] will always have the same value, namely the following:

$$V(T) = K. \quad [2]$$

We can now develop a logical argument as to what the value of the idealized portfolio should be at any time before expiration when t < T. The logic of the argument goes like this.

If you were to buy the portfolio described by [1] at any time before expiration, what would be a fair price for it? We see from [2] that it is guaranteed to be worth K dollars at expiration. Should we be willing to buy it for K dollars? Certainly not. We would be foolish to pay someone K dollars to own a portfolio that will be worth only K dollars several months later. That person would happily take our money and invest it in a riskless, interest-bearing product such as a U.S. treasury bill. At the option's expiration date, they would cash out the treasury bill and use K dollars to buy back the portfolio, while pocketing the interest earned. Thus, we conclude that the true value of the portfolio [1] prior to expiration should be K dollars discounted so as to compensate for the interest it could earn until the options expire. We can express this value of the portfolio as follows:

$$V(t) = K \exp\{- r (T - t)\}, t < T. \quad [3]$$

In [3], r stands for the interest rate associated with the treasury bill, and T − t denotes the amount of time remaining until the options expire. The exp{ } notation denotes the exponential function, which is used to describe the continuous compounding of interest.

We combine [1] and [3] to obtain the put-call parity relationship:

$$C(t) - P(t) = S(t) - K \exp\{-r (T - t)\}, t < T. \quad [4]$$

Now we can apply this put-call parity relationship [4] to demonstrate that calls are more expensive than puts. To fairly compare the prices of the call and put, we want the stock price to coincide with the strike price. That is, we want to make the comparison when S(t) = K. In that special situation, [4] becomes the following:

C(t) – P(t) = K [1 – exp{– r (T–t)}] > 0, t < T.   [5]

Because the right side of [5] is positive, it follows that C(t) > P(t). That is, the price of the call is always greater than the price of the put.

Applications of Put-Call Parity

1. An important application of [4] is the notion of "synthetic stock." As an alternative to buying 100 shares of stock at the strike price K, it is possible to create a synthetic replica of the stock by buying one call contract and selling one put contract with the same strike price K and the same expiration month. How well does this synthetic stock track the real thing? At expiration, when t = T, [4] implies the following:

C(T) – P(T) = S(T) – K.   [6]

That is, the synthetic stock, which has a value of C(T) – P(T) is exactly equal to the profit or loss that results from buying the stock at the strike price K.

This notion of synthetic stock was presented in Chapter 21, "Stock Substitutes." It is particularly appealing because the cost of C(t) – P(t) is relatively small compared to the cost of buying the stock. This means that it is possible to mimic stock performance for a small fraction of the price of real stock. Of course, you must keep in mind that the short put will be viewed as "naked" by your broker, who will require some margin to hold this position.

2. A useful options trade for long-term, buy-and-hold stocks is the "collar trade" using LEAPS. Collar trades are discussed in Chapters 18, "Collars," and 19, "Advanced Collars." In this trade, a stock is purchased for the long term, while an at-the-money LEAPS put is bought to protect the purchase price of the stock and an out-of-the money LEAPS call is sold to

finance the cost of the put. Under the right circumstances, this collar trade can be set up so that there is essentially no risk to your investment, while still allowing for a possible upside profit of 15 percent to 20 percent on an annualized basis.

The riskless aspect of the collar trade is possible because LEAPS calls carry much more time value than LEAPS puts, as implied by [4]. The cash received from selling the more-expensive LEAPS call is used in paying for the relatively inexpensive LEAPS put. It is this disparity in price that allows for a good collar trade.

INDEX

FINANCIAL TIMES

In an increasingly competitive world, it is quality
of thinking that gives an edge—an idea that opens new
doors, a technique that solves a problem, or an insight
that simply helps make sense of it all.

We work with leading authors in the various arenas
of business and finance to bring cutting-edge thinking
and best-learning practices to a global market.

It is our goal to create world-class print publications
and electronic products that give readers
knowledge and understanding that can then be
applied, whether studying or at work.

To find out more about our business
products, you can visit us at www.ftpress.com.